FROM LORD'S TO THE FJORDS

THE SAGA OF ICELANDIC CRICKET

KIT HARRIS

fairfield books

First published by Fairfield Books in 2023

fairfield books

Fairfield Books
Bedser Stand
Kia Oval
London
SE11 5SS

Typeset in Garamond, Proxima Nova and Solaire
Typesetting by Rob Whitehouse
Cover photography by Guðmann Þór Bjargmundsson

This book is printed on paper certified
by the Forest Stewardship Council

Every effort has been made to trace copyright and any oversight
will be rectified in future editions at the earliest opportunity

The views and opinions expressed in this book are those of the author
and do not necessarily reflect the views of the publishers

© 2023 Kit Harris
ISBN 978-1-915237-31-6

A CIP catalogue record for is available from the British Library

Printed by CPI Group (UK) Ltd

For Astrid

FOREWORD

When I was told there is an Iceland cricket team, I thought it was a joke – and, be honest, so did you. When I was informed I'd be interviewing their tour manager on Test Match Special, I assumed it was a leg-pull. Only about halfway through the interview was I convinced that cricket really is played in Iceland.

It seems such an unlikely place. I went there, many moons ago, and was enraptured by the stunning scenery, the hot pools and waterfalls – but it was dark most of the time, and seemed a forbidding and unhospitable environment, not at all suited to the summer game. Then again, I've played cricket in some strange places: on the frozen surface of Lake Geneva, and on the parched dust of the Flinders Ranges in Australia.

It was, unusually, a group of native Icelanders who introduced cricket to their country. That is not quite unique: Afghanistan and Rwanda started that way, and have flourished, lending their own style and interpretation to the game. Perhaps Iceland will be the next success story.

Even so, it seems a stretch to imagine – as this book does – that cricket has a Norse ancestry. But then, there is more Viking in us than we think. I have a condition called Dupuytren's contracture, which makes my fingers curl inwards. The three greatest batsmen of my era – Graham Gooch, David Gower and me – all suffer from it. I was told you must be of Viking descent to have the condition, so if I can boast a Norse heritage, why shouldn't cricket?

Jonathan Agnew
BBC Cricket Correspondent

I
VIKINGS

There are several ways to upset an Icelander. You could ask them if it's dark there for half the year (it isn't). You could mispronounce one of their unpronounceable place names (Fjaðrárgljúfur, anyone?). You could call the tiny Icelandic horse, of which they are unfathomably proud, a 'pony' (it isn't, or at least, they insist it isn't). You could talk about their ancestors as Vikings (the people were the Norse; only the seafaring marauders and pillagers were the Vikings). You could buy a horned helmet at a gift shop (they were dreamed up by the composer Richard Wagner about 600 years after Norse times). Worst of all, you could suggest that Iceland has never done anything of relevance to the rest of the world.

The Icelander will not take kindly to this; you will be berated, and then corrected. An Icelander, you will be told, discovered America (if we overlook the indigenous people who already lived there). Iceland has the first known geyser in the world. Iceland was, in 2009, the first country to be abandoned by McDonalds (the last cheeseburger they sold is on display in a Reykjavík hotel). Iceland was in a football world cup, once, for a bit. This represents, to the Icelanders, a rich culture. As the Reykjavík mayor Jón Gnarr told a press conference in 2010, "we are the people who invented pink mayonnaise and nobody can teach us anything."

And yet it is possible that Iceland's greatest contribution to the modern world has gone unnoticed by the locals, and uncredited by the rest of us. It is an omission I intend to put right. For the Icelanders invented cricket. They don't know it – and be honest, you don't either – but they did. And I will prove it.

According to the official version of things, cricket is an orphan. Its parentage and place of birth are not known; all we seem to be sure about is that its first proven appearance in England was around 1550. We know this because of a legal case in Guildford, in 1598, during which a man named John Derrick testified that he had played cricket as a boy – hence the mid-sixteenth-century estimate.

Derek Birley's *A Social History of English Cricket* hypothesises that the name 'cricket' may have been derived from Middle Dutch words such as *krick* (stick) or *krickstoel* (stool), or the Old French game *criquet*, played at Liettres in 1478. But despite their willingness to entertain ideas of a medieval ancestry in France or Flanders, cricket's historians can do little more than point to Guildford. With apologies to P. G. Wodehouse and Julie Dawn Cole – who played Verruca Salt in *Charlie and the Chocolate Factory* – Guildford is an unexciting birthplace, to say the least.

Let us, then, rescue cricket from this ignominy, and take a look at the Icelandic sagas – the old Norse tales of death and daring, grudges and greed. The sagas aren't entirely works of myth and legend: there is much in their pages that is accurate. They present the historian with a trove of information – much of it supported by archaeological evidence.

Take Reykjavík, for instance. The ancient writing tells us Iceland's first permanent settlement was established in about 874. There was little tangible proof, until a city centre hotel began work on a basement extension in 2001. Excavations turned up a Norse longhouse, and the remains were dated to 871, give or take a few years – and it was exactly where the sagas said it was. It's just that nobody had ever looked before. Indeed, many of the settlements mentioned in the sagas have now been found, and accurately dated. It's clear that, as a historical record, the sagas are not to be sniffed at.

And the sagas don't just tell us where the Norsemen lived, but *how* they lived: how they hunted, how they drank – oh boy, how they drank! – and how they played. It is the last of these that turns up some unexpected information.

Along with hunting, fishing and collecting beautiful trinkets and clothes from their neighbours – Norsemen were nothing if not metrosexual – there was a favourite sport. It was a ball game, called *knattleikr* (translation: 'the ball game'). The Norse were very literal in their nomenclature. Their place names, for instance, are simple descriptions of site and situation (Reykjavík meaning 'smoky bay' and Barnafoss meaning 'the waterfall those children fell into', to give but two examples). *Knattleikr* makes an appearance in no fewer than thirteen of the sagas – all of which were written by different people, in different locations, and sometimes in different centuries.

Most make it clear that *knattleikr* was a contest between bat and ball – the first such in Europe. None of the sagas explain the rules, and we can only glean information about gameplay by cross-referencing the various accounts. Action involving bat and ball appears in eight of them; the other five describe *knattleikr* without mentioning the bat. Here's what we know:

1. A ball is used.
2. A bat is used.
3. The playing area is of defined extent.
4. The ball can go out of play.
5. Players are divided into teams.
6. Each team has a captain.
7. Opposing players face each other in pairs.
8. Players can throw the ball at the person holding the bat.
9. Players can hit the ball with the bat.
10. Players can chase the ball after it has been hit.
11. Players can catch the ball after it has been hit.
12. The game can be played over several days.
13. Tournaments draw huge crowds from all over Iceland.
14. Men argue at length about how the game should be played.

Pretty striking stuff, huh? I mean, as a form of proto-cricket, this is surely worthy of further study, wouldn't you say? Admittedly, there are some features of the game which are less useful for our argument:

1. The game is played on frozen lakes.
2. There is no scoring system; the stronger man wins.
3. Intimidation is a vital ingredient.
4. Either player can be in possession of the ball.
5. Players are sometimes chased when they have the ball.
6. Body contact is allowed.

There are three major differences between *knattleikr* and cricket: the frozen lake, the fighting and contact, and the absence of scores. If I'm going to make a compelling case for cricket descending from the Norse game, I'm going to need to account for those differences. To do that, I need expert help.

Bev Thurber is an ice-skating historian at Shimer College in Illinois. That is, she's an expert on the history of ice skating, not a general historian who likes to skate (and I expect there are far more of the latter than the former). Her paper on the Viking ball game is probably the most thorough general summary of what can be deduced from the sagas. Particularly arresting is her description of the ball as hard, small, light enough to be easily thrown a long distance, but heavy enough to hurt on impact. Archaeological excavations in York turned up Norse balls made from several pieces of leather sewn together. This seems like a promising lead, so I track Dr Thurber down.

Being American, she knows nothing of cricket, but when I show her a cricket ball, she says "it looks about right". But her own theory is that *knattleikr* might be related to lacrosse – the Vikings in North America could have learned it from the native Americans – though she calls it only a glimmer of a link. I'm not convinced. The lacrosse stick has to catch the ball; the *knattleikr* bat (it's called the *knatttré*, by the way, which means 'ball tree') is just for hitting it.

She does help with the frozen lakes, though: Iceland's terrain was exposed rocky lava, or hummocky, marshy turf, neither of which would permit any game involving running, let alone chasing a ball. Any visitor to Iceland soon observes that naturally flat, grassy areas are conspicuous by their absence. A flat, icy surface would have been the best bet (and, for this reason, the playing season began in autumn, after the freeze, but before the snow came). Only on such a surface would the ball's bounce be true. But surely everyone would fall over? Dr Thurber is satisfied that they wouldn't. "They wore spiked shoes," she says. "They were described in detail by the Swedish historian Olaus Magnus in the sixteenth century. Several have been found." Now we're getting somewhere: the Norse invented the small, hard, stitched leather ball *and* spiked footwear.

Having figured out the game's basic characteristics, in terms of action and equipment, it's tempting to try and work out the gameplay – and no one in the world knows more about this than Bill Short of the Viking research organisation, Hurstwic. Dr Short has devoted a substantial portion of his adult life trying to deduce the rules and has recently organised matches. He isn't the first to try. In 1905, an Icelandic historian named Björn Bjarnason (be warned: you are going to have to get used to this sort of name *very* quickly) had a crack at compiling a rule book, but didn't get much right other than the game involving one ball and one bat – he had multiple players going for the ball at the same time, which isn't supported by any of the literature.

Other, more recent, efforts have fared little better. In 1994, Tryggvi Halftrollson of the wonderfully named Society for Creative Anachronism gave each participant a tennis racquet, and awarded a point for getting the ball to the far end of the field of play. In 2003, Danish historian Kåre Johannessen's 'Trelleborg rules' had teams of players, all wielding bats, shooting between goalposts at opposite ends of the field. Roland Ambrose's 'Folcland rules' of 2006 also had teams of bat-wielding players, though they dispensed with goal-scoring (indeed, there seemed to be no obvious point to Ambrose's game at all).

Dr Short's rules, then, are at least the fifth modern code, and while they are no more faithful to the original game than their predecessors – he still has teams facing teams *en masse*, eschewing the one-on-one contest repeatedly described in the sagas – they appear to have caught on in Massachusetts, where Hurstwic operates. In 2007, there was even a New England Intercollegiate Knattleikr Competition.

The game, Dr Short admits, has been 'Americanised' for the sake of sport – and safety. American sports fans demand a method of scoring. They're lost without one – as they are without an abundance of physical caution. Look at how much padding and cladding goes into protecting an American football player. When an American male sees rugby for the first time, he visibly blanches and trembles.

"When we first started out we were scared to death we would hurt somebody," says Dr Short. "But we've only ever injured a spectator." Was that on purpose? "No, a player lost his grip on the bat and it flew out of his hand. There was a lot of blood. But on the whole, people are reasonable about playing the game with an appropriate level of roughness." Apparently, the aim is to get the ball over a goal-line. It all sounds a bit sanitised to me. I'm not sure the Norse would approve, and I say so. "Well, they would approve of some of it, I think," says Dr. Short. "There's an Icelander called Reynir who plays. He's really inventive and always finds ways of getting around you, and getting the ball. And then there's Mike. He's a huge, tall guy, and one time a young boy had the ball, so Mike just picked him up, slung him over his shoulder and carried him over the line."

It seems to me that these attempts to create rules have too often fallen into the trap of assuming a system of scoring is required at all. This may appeal to contemporary notions of sport, but the Norse would have scorned such concepts. Sport, for them, was a show of strength. To hell with a scoreboard: if it wasn't clear to everybody who won, the contest carried on. The Vikings did not play games for points, they played games for ultimate victory: a player played until his opponent could compete no more.

This notion is wholeheartedly supported by the man who knows more about Norse pastimes than any other: Terry Gunnell, professor in folkloristics at the University of Iceland. "*Knattleikr* is a way of fighting without fighting," he says. "The game focuses on upsets. It's never described as an end in itself. It has no relevance in itself, other than advancing the story of the men involved. Its purpose is always to provide the setting for a feud to be resolved."

Once you start poring over the sagas for their *knattleikr* references, two things jump at you. First, the violence. In all the accounts of the game, a total of eight men die during play, and ten more are killed in post-match disagreements. It's enough to make a rugby player squeamish, let alone an American, but in fact murder was one of the game's few *faux pas*. History has preserved only one known rule, laid down by the Grágás (the 'Grey Goose' laws which governed society in Iceland during the Norse period): "Whenever a man goes to play a game, let him stay no longer at it than he pleases. Then he is responsible for himself, as long as any harm he receives was not intended by his opponent. But if he gets lasting injury or death, it is assessed as if it were not a game." Well, that puts the International Cricket Council's disciplinary code into perspective, doesn't it?

The second remarkable thing a saga-reading cricket fan notices is how easy it is to interpret the bat-and-ball action in a 'crickety' way. The bat, the ball and the boundary are obvious. But delve a little deeper and all kinds of familiar occurrences are recognisable: the bowling of bouncers, the big hit over the bowler's head – even the scoring of leg-byes.

THE KNOWN KNATTLEIKR MATCHES

At Hvítá, c. 911. Mýrar v Borg.
Grím wins it for Mýrar in regular play, but Egil
clinches a (literal) sudden-death play-off.

At Esjutjörn, c. 921. Ingjaldsknoll v Foss.
Ingjaldsknoll win thanks to a display of intimidatory bowling by Viglund.

At Seftjörn, c. 960. Hól v Sæból.
Gísli settles a grudge for Hól by thrice felling
Þórgrím and beating him at poetry.

At Seftjörn, c. 960. Hól v Sæból.
Bork breaks Þórstein's bat. The result is unknown
because the reporter is distracted by a poem.

At Miðfjarðarvatn, c. 960. Ós v Reykir.
The young and showy hero, Þórdur, is bested in a battle of verbals.

At Sandi, c. 970. Hvalfjarðarströnd v Botnverjar.
Botnverjar fight back after a tough first day by slaughtering six opponents.

At Ásbjarnarnes, c. 980. Ásbjarnarnes v [Kjartan].
Kjartan plays for the guests against the hosts, and can't be beaten.

At Grímstunga, c. 990. Grímstunga v Hof.
The result is not known, but Ingólfur scores highly with a female spectator.

At Miðfjarðarvatn, c. 1014. Miðfjörður v Auðunarstaðir.
An even game turns into a fight, settled by a kick to the testicles.

At Leikskálavellir, c. 1030. Breiðavík v Álftafjördur.
Blig is banned for having too aggressive a temperament.

At Fjordfylke, Norway. Njorfssons v Víkingssons.
Þórir is annoyed to leave his gloves behind, so murders an opponent.

At Alaborg, Sweden. [Grímur snr] v [Grímur jnr].
The game is a preface to the brutal assassination of King Eystein.

At Jutland, Denmark. Jutland v [Hrafn and Krákur].
A spectator trips a player, who breaks his neck in return.

Square brackets give protagonists' names, where their team is unknown.

The oldest reference is found in *Gull-Þórir's saga*, which dates from the late ninth century, around the time of Iceland's settlement. Young men from four different families are playing *knattleikr* on a frozen fjord. There's no action – it seems just to be casual play – but there is a lively discussion about who should be captain. One set of brothers propose Gull-Þórir, the saga's eponymous hero, since he is the strongest and most accomplished. But the others oppose his appointment for the simple reason that they don't like him. Any cricket fan – hell, any sports fan – can think of a modern equivalent. How many of us have played for a team in which the best player is automatically granted the position of captain? How many of us have thought the captain to be a dickhead?

The earliest description of an actual game – and by far the most memorable – comes in *Egil's saga*. Egil is perhaps the greatest antihero in ancient European literature. He is a poet, a sorcerer, and a farmer – but above all, he is a bastard. His inability to behave with even the slightest civility to anyone he meets is best illustrated when he is a guest at the home of a man named Armod. Armod treats Egil and his men to as much meat and ale as they can consume and, not unusually for that time – or indeed for this – the drinking becomes competitive. The lightweights are considered to be lacking in masculinity, and there is honour in being the last man standing. One by one, Egil's men fall into a stupor, while Egil finishes his ale, and then theirs. Eventually, he succumbs. He rises unsteadily, staggers over to his host, and:

> He grabbed Armod by the shoulders and shoved him against
> a post. Then Egil vomited copiously all over Armod's face, in
> his eyes, up his nose and into his mouth. Armod breathed in
> the vomit and choked on it. Then he, too, vomited everywhere.
> Armod's servants exclaimed that Egil was disgusting; only an
> awful person would do such a thing; vomiting should be done
> outside. Egil replied: "Don't you start. I'm no worse than your
> master. Look, he's spewing his guts just like me." Then Egil
> went back to his seat and demanded more drink.

It will not surprise you to learn that Egil's participation in the ball game between Borg and Mýrar in 911 is not a study in refined sportsmanship. The contest takes place by the river Hvítá in south Iceland. Teams were customarily divided not only geographically, but along family lines: Borg's team is assembled by Egil's father, and Egil demands to be selected. Once the game begins, Egil faces a youth called Grím, who is older and stronger than him. Grím soon dominates. Egil loses his cool and hits him with the bat, but Grím pins him to the ground and warns him: "You'd better learn how to behave, or you'll suffer." Egil leaves the game in a sulk, jeered by the Mýrar players. But he finds a sympathetic listener in his captain (the captain tended to be a senior member of the family, rather than the star player), who hands Egil an axe and sends him back to the field, where Grím is still showboating. Egil runs up to him and drives the axe into his head "right down to the brain". Then, showing remarkable sang-froid, even for Vikings, Egil and his captain simply walk back to their camp. What's more remarkable still is that the boy they've just slain is eleven years old, and Egil is only seven. Grím's team-mates are understandably somewhat cross. A battle ensues, and seven more men are killed. If this is the first recorded playing of the earliest form of cricket, I think you'll agree it's a cracker.

About a decade later, in *Víglund's saga*, a two-day game is played. This is not by any means the only example of a multi-day contest: spectators came from all over the country, camped next to the field of play, and expected a good deal of sport for their trouble. Víglund bats for Ingjaldsknoll against Foss. Jökull has the ball. It's an age-old tale of intimidating bowling gone wrong. A particularly big hit incurs Jökull's wrath, and the next ball hits Víglund in the face, cutting his eyebrow. When the game resumes the following day, the players' roles are reversed: with his first ball, Viglund wounds Jökull in turn; with his second, he knocks him out cold, settling the matter.

Gísli's saga, from the mid-tenth century, has the longest description of a contest; in fact, we're treated to two games which might, to put it mildly, be described as grudge matches. Specifically, Þórgrím (of Sæból) is pitted against his brother-in-law Gísli (from Hól), having recently murdered Gísli's brother. To add even more spice, the game is played in the shadow of the dead man's burial mound. Given the context, the crowd is understandably large. Nobody is quite sure who will win; public opinion tends to lean towards Gísli, since his family has been wronged, giving him greater motivation. But the early exchanges are even. Gísli's other brother is concerned. "Word is going round that you're not giving your all," he says. Gísli is phlegmatic: "We haven't been fully proven against each other yet. But we're leading up to it."

They certainly were. The game continues, and Gísli starts to get the upper hand. Then, says the saga, he "brought Þórgrím down and the ball went out of play". Now, granted, this might sound like a rough tackle close to the touchline. But to a connoisseur of cricket, it's clear what happened: Gísli bowled a short-pitched ball which hit Þórgrím on the head and ran away to the boundary for four leg-byes. The four leg-byes aren't mentioned, of course; finer points of cricket, such as scoring bonus runs after being hit by the ball, are the sort of genteel invention with which the English habitually ruined games of brute force and strength. A true Viking didn't want leg-byes, he wanted blood.

Þórgrím is not impressed. As Gísli goes to fetch the ball, Þórgrím reaches out and holds him back, only to be thrown to the floor again. The saga goes into detail: "He could do nothing to break his fall. His knuckles were grazed, blood rushed from his nose and the flesh was scraped from his knees." As the English would say, this is definitely not cricket. But then again, it's not exactly football, golf or tenpin bowling, either. *Knattleikr* routinely gets out of hand. Þórgrím picks himself up from the dust and steels himself. He looks over at the burial mound and recalls – in traditional skaldic poetry – how he slayed Gísli's brother: "The spear screeched his wound, sorely. I cannot be sorry." Gísli hears this and is incensed. He bowls again, even faster. This time, Þórgrím is struck between the shoulder blades, and falls on his face again. Gísli triumphantly declares: "The ball smashed his shoulders, broadly. I cannot be sorry either." Everyone agrees that the victory is emphatic, since Gísli has not only brought his opponent down three times, but also trumped him in skaldic verse. Triumph by stanza, as well as strength.

The verbals weren't always quite so eloquent. In *Þórdur's saga*, set at broadly the same time, the star of the story plays for his farmstead, Ós, in place of his uncle, who is said to be "getting on a bit". Þórdur is very young, but fells his opponent, Ásbjörn of Reykir, with great force, and exclaims: "The cesspool pig has fallen!" No sooner has he said it, than Ásbjörn lands a much harder blow, retorting: "Not really ready to play against grown-ups, are you, bum-fluff?"

15

Back to *Gísli's saga*, for the second instalment. Sæból demand a rematch, with Þórgrím's brother Börk to the fore. Hól put up Þórstein, a friend of Gísli's. He proves to be very strong with the bat, and Börk "made no headway against him all day" despite trying everything (modern bowlers are permitted to sympathise – though not too much, since Börk is the bad guy, remember). Börk eventually loses his temper, grabs the bat, and breaks it in two. This is appalling behaviour, even by Norse standards. Now comes another gesture which was as meaningful back then as it would be now. Gísli takes his friend's broken bat and sets about repairing it – but hands Þórstein his own bat so he can conclude the game. What we want to happen next is for Þórstein to beat Börk – either in regular game play or just by beating him to a pulp – but the result is not recorded because the author is distracted by a particularly good poem recited by Gísli and forgets all about the game. All we get is "the game came to an end and Þórstein went home". There's an arresting coda, though: "As the men made their way home from the game, they began to talk and debate about how it should be played, and eventually they began to argue." Men, I suppose, will always be men. No doubt the Norse enjoyed these debates all the more when they were pissed, which was of course often. The present discussion concludes when Þórstein is hit with an axe, and runs home to his mother, who is said to be "displeased about what had befallen him." Mothers, I suppose, will always be mothers.

The game's violence seems to reach its peak in about 970, when *Hörður's saga* describes a match, played on sand, between Botnverjar and Hvalfjarðarströnd. This contest could be said to hold three cricketing records: the first player draft, the first instance of match-fixing, and the highest death toll. The match manager, Kolgrímur, fixes the player selections so that Hvalfjarðarströnd have by far the stronger team. Botnverjar get off to a bad start and are already in a losing position by the end of the first day's play. The hero, Hörður, exhorts them not to give up. His team-talk proves inspiring: next morning, his players slay six of their opponents.

A little later, in *Laxdæla saga*, another selector is similarly unscrupulous. Hallur owns a farmstead in north Iceland. According to the text, "A stauncher man was not to be found in all of the northern quarter." He entertains an equally strong man, Kjartan, and asks if he plays *knattleikr*. Kjartan replies: "I haven't had much practice recently." Yeah, pull the other one, mate. We've all heard that before. Hallur organises the teams and puts all the strongest players in one team – against Kjartan. But Kjartan repels everything they can throw at him, "but no man had either the strength nor the stamina to cope with him".

In *Hallfreður's saga*, which takes place before the turn of the century, we are introduced to a hero of a different kind. The people of Grímstunga hold an autumn party and invite their neighbours from Hof. Among the guests is Ingólfur, who is a noted player – and, if you get my drift, a noted player. The women of Grímstunga particularly enjoy watching him play, and he seems to like the attention. At one point, he accidentally-on-purpose throws the ball out of bounds, and towards the spectators. One of them, Valgerður, picks up the ball and stuffs it under her clothes. Ingólfur runs up and asks for the ball. "You threw it, so you find it," returns Valgerður. Sensing a pursuit more alluring than the game, Ingólfur sits down next to her and they talk all day. It is not known what they did all night.

Set in 1014, the game in *Grettir's saga* is a big event, and draws crowds from far and wide. Marquees are set up around the ground, and there is much drinking over the days of the tournament (think Tunbridge Wells, but without the rhododendrons). Grettir's brother insists on enlisting him for the Miðfjörður team, and Grettir finds himself facing Auðun from Viðidalur. An outlaw from Norway, Grettir is impetuous and aggressive, but Auðun is seven years Grettir's senior, not to mention stronger, and a superb batter. He hits the ball back over Grettir's head – a humiliation for any bowler – and Grettir is forced to retrieve it. With his next ball, Grettir hits Auðun on the head and draws blood. Now it is Auðun's turn to feel humiliated, and he strikes Grettir with the bat. Inevitably, things go downhill from there. There is much grappling and wrestling (the onlookers are impressed that Grettir is much stronger than they'd thought). Eventually, Grettir loses his balance and stumbles, whereupon Auðun deals what is apparently the decisive blow by kneeing Grettir – who is fourteen, by the way – in the balls. Fortunately, there is no long-term damage to future relations (other than, presumably, those issuing from Grettir's testicles), since the combatants are from the same family, and nobody wants a full-blown feud. The tale ends in typically prosaic fashion: "The game went on as before and nothing else caused any friction."

The mid-eleventh century's *Eyrbyggja saga* provides further insight into the game, without going into details about any particular contest. Again, the similarities with cricket and its characters are striking. A multi-day tournament takes place in west Iceland, under the Öxl mountain, whose playing field is notable for having a players' pavilion (indeed, the field is called Leikskálavellir, or 'The Playing Field with a Players' Pavilion'). It is large enough to accommodate spectators overnight. Altogether, it seems as though *knattleikr* has passed a watershed, becoming more focused and better organised, and moving away from unbridled violence. The saga even makes a point of saying: "A good supply of fit men played, except Blíg, who did not participate on account of his aggressive temperament."

Until now, a player with a touch of the homicidal had been regarded as something of an asset. But matters of selection had become more sensitive: the brothers Björn and Arnbjörn, from Breiðavík, are such good players that it's considered unfair for them to play on the same team. The opposing team, Álftafjörður, are less inclined to be sporting: they send their slave to murder one of the Breiðavík players under cover of darkness, but as he creeps into the pavilion, he trips over a loose tassel, and "there was a huge thud as if the skinned carcass of a cow had been thrown on the floor." The slave is clapped in irons, and the Breiðavík men press him to spill the beans – then kill him anyway.

So far, we have amassed a great deal of information about *knattleikr*, and – if you interpret it a certain way – good reason to consider it the forerunner of cricket. The trouble is, everything's set in Iceland. We've reached the middle of the eleventh century, and we have four hundred years to get the game to the border of France and Belgium. Three of the later sagas are going to get it there.

Most of the characters in the sagas came from mainland Scandinavia, travelling to Iceland in the name of trades (and raids). But there is sporting action on the continent, too. In *Þórstein's saga*, a game takes place between the hero's family and the grandsons of King Ólaf of Norway. Þórstein's oldest brother Þórir finds himself bowling at Ólaf, the king's second-oldest grandson. Þórir hurls "the ball on the ground so hard that it bounded over Ólaf and pitched far behind him." The spectators believe the game to be over, pack up their things, and begin to leave. It's not entirely clear what's happened, but a modern cricket fan might recall a controversial incident in Australia's Big Bash League in 2021. The Sydney Sixers needed one run to win, and their star batter James Vince had scored 98. If he could hit the next ball off the field, his team would win and he'd reach a coveted hundred. But the Perth Scorchers' bowler, Andrew Tye, deliberately hurled down a ball so far out of Vince's reach that it couldn't be hit – thus conceding a wide, adding a run, and concluding the match with Vince unable to reach three figures.

Is this what Þórir did to Ólaf? Did he deliberately send the ball so high over Ólaf's head that he couldn't hit it? Thus robbing him of the glory of making the winning hit? Perhaps not – but one way or another, Ólaf is furious about it, and hits Þórir on the head with the bat. In the post-game melee, Þórir leaves his gloves behind, and is determined go back to the playing field to fetch them. When he gets there, he sees Ólaf, and stabs him to death.

There are references to *knattleikr* later being played in the territory of King Eystein, at the lost fort of Alaborg. This was perhaps in Sweden or Finland, or possibly even in Russia. *Hálfdán's saga* describes a game being played, for the benefit of the King, between two shipwrecked Russian men, both named Grímur. The elder proves the stronger and hits the ball beyond the boundary; the younger Grímur runs to fetch it, only to find it has rolled underneath a spectator's chair. The queen's chair, in fact. Grímur crawls under her chair on all fours, retrieves the ball and then pauses to whisper in the queen's ear. Whatever he says makes her blush. King Eystein asks her what the young man said, but she won't tell. When darkness falls, the king is murdered in his bedchamber – the queen having conveniently left the room for a few moments.

And then we have *Hrólf's saga*, which gets us as far south as Denmark. Two brothers, Hrafn and Krákur, arrive at the hall of Earl Þorgný of Jutland. They look strong, and brag about how tough they are to beat with bat and ball. The Earl's team, though, are considered the best in Denmark, so the brothers are invited to form a team to play their hosts. Over several days of play, Hrafn and Krákur prove an irresistible force with the ball, hitting some opponents, knocking down others, and breaking three players' arms. Desperate to avoid humiliation, the battered locals beg the Earl's son Stefnir to play. Stefnir is a mountain of a man, and calls upon Hrólf, the saga's hero, to join in.

The next day's play begins and, as before, the brothers quickly establish the upper hand. Eventually, Stefnir and Hrólf come together, and the tables are turned: Hrafn and Krákur are forced to chase the ball around at length. The relieved spectators find their voice and begin to jeer the visitors. Hrafn, fielding the ball on the boundary, is deliberately tripped by one of the onlookers; enraged, he breaks the man's neck. Earl Þorgný calls upon his men to kill Hrafn and Krákur, but Hrólf establishes they are Flemish men of high birth, and they are pardoned.

Flemish men! That means they played *knattleikr* in Flanders. Remember that early reference to *criquet*, in Liettres? Did we just get proto-cricket from Iceland to Flanders, in time for 1478?

I return to Professor Gunnell, hoping to close the gap in the chronology. He is sceptical. For a start, he says, the Norse likely gave up on pastimes. "By 1264 the temperature in Europe was falling fast," he says. "People were focusing solely on survival. Everyone looked after their own. Icelandic communities weren't towns or harbours, they were farms. There was a lot less socialising. And the chieftains who ruled Iceland by then – well, they weren't easy-going. They were like *The Sopranos*. Everyday life became increasingly difficult."

Professor Gunnell suspects *knattleikr* could be related to the Irish sport of hurling – and that the Vikings might have picked it up on the way to Iceland. He has even written an academic paper espousing his theory. I attempt a counterargument. "In hurling, all the players have a stick, and they pass the ball to each other," I begin. "In *knattleikr*, it's a player with a ball throwing it at a player with a bat. It's one-on-one. Cricket's a much better fit." Professor Gunnell remains unconvinced. "Well, with hurling you have a possible mechanism for it travelling west with the Vikings," he says. "How does cricket travel east from Iceland?"

I tell him I think *knattleikr* could have got to Flanders. He bridles a little. "But there's no evidence of it taking place outside Iceland," he protests. "Well, we've got Þórir and Ólaf in Sweden," I reply. "And then we've got Stefnir and Hrólf in Denmark, playing against those two lads from Flanders. What about them?" Professor Gunnell gives me a long look. For a moment I think he is worried. "But the Vikings were so uncrickety," he says.

II

OCCUPIED

What we did for the world was two things. We wrote the Sagas: the history of Norway, Sweden, Denmark, Orkney as well as the Faroe Islands. They did the fighting, while we went along and wrote the history. We kept the records of everything the Nordic nations know about their history before the thirteenth century. The other thing we did was create a society without state authority during the times of the Icelandic Commonwealth until 1264. Since then, we've done nothing that matters for over 700 years. Other than possibly the financial crash of 2008, nothing we've done has any meaning to the rest of the world. And why should it? We're a minuscule country.

Dr Ásgeir Jónsson, Governor of the Bank of Iceland, 2019

1264 was a big year for Iceland. Until then, the country had been divided into Norse farmsteads, each ruled by a chieftain, all of whom came to an annual Parliament. They had law, they had independence, and they had cricket. Everything changed when, facing falling temperatures and rising conflicts, the chieftains agreed to put their island under the protective wing of Norway. Sweden joined the alliance and, eventually, so did Denmark. Into the dark ages went the so-called Kalmar Union, until infighting prompted Norway and Sweden to go off on their own in 1523, leaving Denmark to do what it liked with Iceland.

Dr Jónsson's appraisal may seem a trifle harsh, but he really does have a point. The Danes treated Iceland as little more than a remote trading post which, for a couple of centuries, wasn't allowed to do business with anyone other than Denmark. Iceland was considered, in effect, a grubby cold-storage warehouse at the end of the garden. Little was given, and much taken.

It is hard to exaggerate just how tough life was for the Icelanders, and how hardy they became. A volcanic eruption in 1783 killed thousands, wiped out 80 per cent of the livestock, and brought about a biblical famine. In the battle for survival, progress was hard enough to come by, let alone recreation. There was no Renaissance, nothing even remotely noteworthy in terms of arts or sciences. Iceland's culture, economy and infrastructure remained steadfastly and miserably medieval. Only in the late nineteenth century, when Denmark began the process of devolution, did Iceland begin to modernise. The wheel was not used until 1863, before which it would have served no purpose, since even the busiest thoroughfares were coarse, rocky paths. Just two brick houses were built in Iceland in the entire nineteenth century. There were no roads outside the capital city before 1900. Only when a semblance of modernity came to Iceland did local people find there was time to do anything other than exist.

Football appeared at the turn of the twentieth century, when the first three clubs were formed: Reykjavík FC in the western part of the city, Fram FC in the eastern part, and – somewhat incongruously – Vestmannaeyjar FC on a tiny island off the south coast, a five-hour boat trip from the capital. Football took the population by storm, especially the young. On the evening of 21 April 1908, a group of 32 schoolboys crammed into the basement of a house on Túngata in Reykjavík and signed a resolution establishing Iceland's fourth football club, Vikings FC. The founding members were barely older than the century: the newly elected chairman was twelve years old, the treasurer was eleven and the secretary was nine. The first motion they passed was to begin raising money to fund the purchase of a football.

Reykjavík and Fram were a few steps ahead – they already had footballs, for a start – and in 1911 they clubbed together to acquire and flatten a piece of land called Melarnir ('The Gravels'), just to the south of the city centre, for use as Iceland's first sports ground. It was no more than swept grit, but for a country strewn with jagged lava rocks and beset by boggy marshland, it was nothing short of a luxury. The workmen hired to clear the land, on being told about the sport for which it was intended, were so intrigued they decided to form their own club on the spot. They named it Valur ('Falcon') FC, because one swooped over their heads as they shook hands on the plan.

The first season of the Icelandic football league was played at Melarnir in 1912. There were just three teams: Reykjavík, Fram and

Vestmannaeyjar. Valur weren't invited, on the basis that, though they had formed a club, they did not yet know how to play football; Vikings were excluded because their oldest player was just thirteen. Vestmannaeyjar endured a terrible sea voyage home after their first game and withdrew from the league with seasickness (they didn't dare play another away fixture until 1926). Valur were deemed good enough to participate by 1915. Vikings, still all teenagers, were admitted in 1918, and beat Valur 5–0 in their first game. Within three years, they had won the league.

Perhaps unsurprisingly, Iceland's first international football opponents were Denmark, who visited in 1919 for a five-match series. Still less surprisingly, Iceland were trounced in the first four games, but then fate – and a little Viking-style mischief – dealt them a lucky hand. Before the final match, the Danish players were taken on a long horse ride, shown the sights, and plied with drink. Very much the worse for wear, and in appalling weather, they lost the game. The Icelanders were jubilant: they'd proved that – under certain circumstances, and with the odds substantially and deliberately stacked in their favour – they could come out on top. This was all the encouragement they needed.

Iceland had only a couple of Olympians: a runner and a wrestler who went to Stockholm in 1912. There was little money available for sport. A proper stadium, Melavöllur ('Gravel Field') was built on top of the gravel in 1926, and the pitch was upgraded from grit to dirt, but there was still no grass sports field anywhere in the country.

Still, when Adolf Hitler undertook to pay the expenses of all participants in the Berlin Olympics of 1936, the Icelanders felt this was the moment they had been waiting for: the debut of an Icelandic team on the biggest stage. The bad news was that only sixteen teams were invited to participate in the football event – and Iceland wasn't one of them. Icelandic sports were entirely amateur, and here was the chance of a lifetime: all-expenses-paid entry to the Olympics for their entire national team – if only they had a national team in something other than football. So they did what any ambitious country would do in that situation: they gritted their teeth, crossed their fingers and chose water polo.

Only about two dozen Icelanders played water polo. Not many more could even swim. But even by the 1930s, the modern Icelandic attitude – that it's highly unlikely that anyone can be better at anything than an Icelander – had taken hold. They lost all their matches heavily, but it remains the national water polo team's best Olympic performance, not least because they never entered again.

Hitler turned out to be the unlikely catalyst for the first appearance of modern cricket in Iceland, by virtue of starting World War Two. The War wasn't supposed to visit Iceland: it had no armed forces of any kind and was determined to remain neutral. There were two difficulties with such a position. The first was that Iceland was still a territory of Denmark, and since Denmark had been occupied by the Nazis in 1940, and the Faroe Islands hastily seized by the British three days later, there seemed little hope of Iceland keeping its head out of the fray. The second difficulty was Iceland's strategic location in the middle of the ocean. A foothold in Iceland might lead to control over the Atlantic.

The British sent two cruisers and two destroyers, with nearly 800 men aboard, to seize Iceland in May 1940. The announcement of the occupation was typically British; their welcome typically Icelandic: the only battle was for the title of 'most understated gesture'. A local policeman spotted the fleet of unfamiliar boats arriving in the dead of night and ran back to the police hut to tell his boss. The chief, a pragmatic man called Einar Arnalds, felt he ought to make his own appraisal of the situation before waking the Foreign Minister, so rode his bicycle down to the waterfront with his binoculars. Having satisfied himself that the ships were indeed foreign, he telephoned the Minister.

"A number of enemy ships have been sighted from the harbour, sir," said Arnalds.

The Minister was equally practically minded.

"Who's that? Do you know what time it is?" Naturally, as a politician, he liked to be apprised of all the facts.

"It's Einar, sir. Your chief of police."

"Who's been sighted at the harbour?"

"Enemy ships, sir. Four of them."

A pause, no doubt. The answer to the next question would have a critical influence on decision-making.

"Where are they from?" asked the Minister. "Are they British or German?"

"They're British," said Arnalds. "Probably. Sir."

"Then it can wait until breakfast."

As the Minister returned to his slumbers, Arnalds went back to the harbour to find a sizeable crowd had arrived – as had the British ambassador. When the ships had docked, their officers were impatient to disembark. Few of their men had found their sea-legs. Sick streamed across the deck. The gangplank was lowered and the British disembarked, much to the indignation of the locals. One seized a marine's rifle, stuffed a cigarette in the barrel and tossed it back to him.

"Be careful where you point that thing, soldier boy."

An officer marched up and told the marine to stop fooling around with the natives. There were more pressing matters to attend to – not least, a formal declaration of occupation, which was done by pinning a note to the door of the post office, announcing that Iceland was now under British authority.

After a year or so, the British handed control to the Americans, even though the United States had not yet entered the War. For the remainder of the conflict, the British maintained two Royal Air Force stations between the slopes of Öskjuhlíð, a forested hill to the south of the city, near Melavöllur stadium. By the summer of 1943, these stations were manned by Nos. 120, 190, 251 and 269 Squadrons. British Royal Navy ships regularly visited Reykjavík; during August, *HMS Glasgow* was docked at the harbour, and the seamen challenged the airmen to two cricket matches at Melavöllur.

Stationed in the RAF in Iceland at that time was a cricketer named Cecil Wigglesworth, who played a first-class match at The Oval in London in 1927. Air Commodore Wrigglesworth is believed by many to be the inspiration for Biggles, the adventurous fictional pilot created by W. E. Johns. Also serving at the base was Flight Lieutenant John Crompton Lamburn, the younger brother of Richmal Crompton, and the boy on whom her *Just William* stories were based.

The writer and cricketer Charlie Connelly was thrilled to discover this literary connection and amused himself with the thought of Biggles calling William for a quick single among the volcanoes. In fact, neither played. Crompton Lamburn had fallen ill with a peptic ulcer which would see him invalided out of the RAF the following month; Wigglesworth was 49, and possibly pipped by younger men in the rush for places.

And a rush there certainly was. When the match invitation arrived on the *Glasgow*, Surgeon-Lieutenant Dave Rice was appointed manager and was overwhelmed with volunteers, not only from his own ship, but also from *HMS Berwick* alongside. There was one automatic choice. The *Berwick* counted among its officers no less a cricketer than Captain Norman Grace, the son of E. M. Grace, and thus the nephew of W. G. Grace, the greatest cricketer to have played the game up to that point. Captain Grace had already played three first-class matches for the Navy, against the Army, and had bowled well. Like his father and uncle, his stock-in-trade was canny slows. He, surely, would be the Navy's secret weapon – and the star attraction.

Rice not only had great cricketing skill at his disposal, but great valour too. Lieutenant George Phillips had been awarded the Distinguished Service Cross for gallantry during the Dieppe Raid the previous year. Lieutenant Peter Davies would be similarly decorated in 1945, for his courage in sweeping mines from the Atlantic swell.

The RAF were not to be outdone in terms of bravery. Their team included a flying ace, Wing Commander Leslie Peacock, who'd flown a DH9 bomber in World War One. And from No. 120 Squadron, on detachment to Reykjavík from February 1943, they had Flight Lieutenant Douglas Fleming-Williams, and a New Zealander, Warrant Officer Bryan Turnbull, both of whom registered U-boat hits within a fortnight of arriving in Iceland. No. 120 Squadron destroyed fourteen German submarines during the War, and Turnbull – who sank four of them – received the Distinguished Flying Cross.

Rice was evidently something of a cricketing impresario. He discovered that the Admiral of the *Glasgow* had, on a whim before departure, stashed a complete set of cricket gear in the ship's stores. He also battled with the intransigent Icelandic authorities by gaining their consent to stage the match at Melavöllur (it could hardly have been played anywhere else). The Icelanders reluctantly gave their assent on two conditions: first, that it was understood that the loan of the stadium should not be misinterpreted as support for the Allied occupation; second, that under no circumstances would this "strange game" cause holes to be poked into their much-prized and carefully neglected quintessence of dirt.

Thursday 12 August dawned bright and sunny, dispelling the fears of the more weather-weary airmen that it would snow. The boatswain's store was raided for a strip of coconut matting, which acted as the pitch; Rice won the toss and sent the RAF in. Rice himself bowled the first ball to Flight Lieutenant R. M. Mitchell, an Australian, who hooked it to the boundary. The English spectators cheered, the Icelanders looked baffled, and the American servicemen – lovers of sport but unexposed to cricket – pitched in with cries of "Let's go!" and "Get that ball in!" Rice settled into an accurate spell, but the Antipodean pair of Mitchell and Turnbull plundered 87 in the first half-hour – hitting five sixes – and were particularly harsh on the minesweeper Davies, whose two overs cost 38. It was Grace who broke the partnership with a return catch off Mitchell.

The Americans then got what they had come for, as Rice sent the leg stump flying. They leaped to their feet, shouting "Railway!" Now it was the Englishmen's turn to be confused, until someone explained it was a baseball expression meaning "drop him from the team".

Grace snared Turnbull, one short of his half-century, then sent back the veteran Peacock. Rice uprooted the leg stump again, but the sixth-wicket pair added 32, and 163 for 7 was reckoned to be a good score.

The Navy's chase began slowly. They lost their first wicket at 19 but Rice led the way with three sixes in a second-wicket stand worth 61. His swashbuckling 69 was the top score of the match, made in three-quarters of an hour, but when Mitchell castled him, and trapped Grace immediately afterwards, the pursuit seemed impossible. Still the seamen went for it, determined to do or die. Turnbull and Mitchell plugged away, aided by three careless run-outs, and the last eight batters went for the addition of just 15. The RAF won by 24 runs.

In the absence of competitive cricket back in England, *The Cricketer* published scores and a match report, observing that the RAF were remarkably good at fielding "considering their lack of practice". It also noted that the Navy may have been hamstrung by the problem of selecting from such a large number of volunteers: "A team finally being formed of the keenest but, alas, not the most skilful cricketers!" Indeed, other than himself and Grace, it looks as though Rice had nothing. A second match was played two weeks later, apparently with a considerably higher standard of play, but without the novelty value of the first; it was not recorded for posterity. The coverage in *The Cricketer* ends in a somewhat hackneyed tone: "We went away happy in the knowledge that this king of all games had extended his sovereignty and hoisted his flag in far-off Iceland." Clearly the reporter had never heard of *knattleikr*.

Combat honours aside, it was arguably Rice who lived the most remarkable life. He had already bowled for the Navy against the Army at Lord's in 1942, dismissing Denis Compton, perhaps England's finest post-war batter. On returning from service in Iceland, he played in the same fixture in 1944, and represented the Navy against a combined Australian Services team at Portsmouth in 1945, taking a catch to dismiss the legendary Lindsay Hassett for 189. Rice retired from the Navy in 1957, but the cricket continued. In 1958, aged 44, he made his first-class debut for Col. L. C. Stevens' XI against the touring New Zealanders; he captained the XI in 1960 and 1961, when it featured England greats Len Hutton and Tom Graveney. He specialised in psychiatry and pioneered the use of lithium to treat manic depression.

Not all the players survived the war. Wing Commander Richard Longmore, whose 22 runs propelled the RAF to their imposing total, was the leader of No. 120 squadron. Seven weeks after the match, on 4 October, he was accompanying an Allied convoy across the Atlantic, when it was attacked by the German U-539. Longmore dropped depth charges, and damaged the submarine, but his Liberator was shot down. No trace of the aircraft or its crew was found.

The post-war decades cemented the modern Icelandic character: proud, conservative, and wary of outsiders – not just of their presence, but of their character and influence. Iceland was a founder member of NATO in 1949, so soon after the American military departed the island, they returned. The locals were unconvinced of the desirability of joining NATO, and unimpressed by the Americans, whom they regarded as noisy, outspoken, brash and bawdy. Worse, they brought alcohol, guitar music and lewd dancing. Icelanders had been weaned on the literary tradition, with its tales of stoicism and heroism, and they disdained the raw, uninhibited culture of the transatlantic visitors. They tolerated the Americans for the attractiveness of their money – and, in some cases, of their men.

ICELAND'S FIRST CRICKET MATCH

RAF v Navy at Melavöllur on 12 August 1943

RAF innings

Ft.-Lt. R. M. Mitchelll	c and b Grace	37
W/O B. W. Turnbull	lbw b Grace	49
P/O J. C. G. Wilmott	b Rice	4
Sqd-Ldr. J. Heath	b Rice	6
Wing-Cmd. L. W. D. Peacock	c Rice b Grace	1
F/O N. F. Wallis	not out	16
Wing-Cmd. R. M. Longmore	c and b Barnes	22
F/Lt. D. C. Fleming-Williams	b Barnes	6
F/O I. J. Inglis		
P/O S. I. Evans		
P/O C. S. Page		
	Extras	22
	for 7 wickets, declared	**163**

Rice 8–2–36–2, Davies 2–0–38–0, Grace 7–0–55–3, Barnes 2–0–11–2.

Navy innings

Lt. G. K. Eastwood	c Inglis b Fleming-Williams	37
Lt. G. J. Cialis	b Page	6
Surg-Lt. D. Rice	b Mitchell	69
Capt. N. V. Grace	lbw b Mitchell	0
Lt. P. E. Davies	run out	3
Lt. D. F. Barnes	st Longmore b Turnbull	2
Pay-Lt. H. J. C. Cotter	not out	3
Lt. M. M. Moyes	b Turnbull	2
Surg-Lt. L. S. Anderson	c and b Mitchell	2
Sub-Lt. G. S. Phillips	run out	5
Pay-Lt. C. A. Bolton	run out	0
	Extras	10
	all out	**139**

Page 5–0–27–1, Heath 3–0–6–0, Fleming-Williams 3–0–42–1, Mitchell 4–0–25–3, Turnbull 2–0–15–2.

Initially, fraternising with the Americans was strictly prohibited. Though the war was over, they were still widely seen as an occupying force. The Americans longed to visit the city when not on duty, but the Reykjavík authorities were vehemently against it. Eventually, an agreement was reached that the troops could go to town on Wednesday nights – but the municipal council then banned the sale of alcohol on Wednesdays. This discouraged many servicemen from making the hour-long journey to the capital, and they instead concentrated their attentions on the nearby village of Keflavík. It became the unlikely birthplace of Iceland's rock and roll scene – and even today, it is the only place in Iceland where basketball flourishes.

The Americans' continued presence became known as 'The Situation'. For a while, the local police kept a file on several hundred women believed to be having sexual relations with the troops. A woman thus suspected was branded a traitor or prostitute; the authorities grimly recorded that the liaisons resulted in 332 marriages and 255 children, referred to as *ástandsbörn*, or 'Children of the Situation'.

For centuries, Icelanders had been left to their own devices, and now it seemed that as soon as they were relieved of the Danish yoke, they had fallen under the influence of the Americans. Foreigners, it was felt, could be accepted – even welcomed, through gritted teeth – if they brought their money on holiday for a short while. If they made suitable noises of appreciation of the land's wild beauty, or acknowledge its cultural superiority, so much the better. But Iceland was for the Icelanders; visitors could look and admire, but not share.

While a cultural and social revolution swept across the Western world in the 1950s and 1960s, Iceland's outlook remained austere. They kept themselves very much to themselves. There was no upper class, no aristocracy, and no political class. The politicians represented the people because they were *part* of the people: anti-Europe, financially shrewd and broadly nationalist. The two main political parties, the Independents and the Progressives, were both to the right of centre, and almost indistinguishable in ideology or policy. Little has changed in this regard: one or other of these parties has been in power for all but five years since full independence came in 1944. Iceland was its own inspiration, its own reward.

Every now and then, there was a chance to show the world just how powerful the 'little guy' could be, even against apparently overwhelming odds. Between 1958 and 1976, the Icelandic government made a series of unilateral proclamations extending its sea territory (and the exclusive fishing rights therein) from four to 200 nautical miles around its coastline. The British, used to having as much sea as they wanted, were furious, and sent in the Royal Navy: 22 frigates, seven supply vessels and six defence tugs, all heavily armed. The Icelanders had six coastguard boats equipped with large scissors for cutting the nets of the British fishing boats. Every time the Icelanders extended their territory, the UK protested to the United Nations. Every time, the United Nations sided with Iceland. The Icelanders just love it when a plucky underdog wins – as long as that underdog is Iceland. The England football team were, of course, to be reminded of this several decades later.

One foreign interloper who *did* gain a foothold in Iceland was an Englishman named Peter Salmon, who immigrated in October 1979 to marry a local called Ólöf Guðmundsdóttir. Salmon was a man of cricket and a man of Kent, and of the three dozen wedding guests, 22 were members of St Lawrence and Highland Court Cricket Club. Salmon's club-mates organised a cricket match for the stag evening, and managed to secure the use of Melavöllur just as Surgeon-Lieutenant Rice had done 36 years previously.

Someone tipped off the national press. The morning newspaper, *Morgunblaðið* 'The Morning Paper' and the daily paper, *Dagblaðið* 'The Daily Paper' sent reporters and photographers to cover the match on 20 October. It made the front pages.

"When my friends heard I was getting married in Iceland, they thought it would be a great chance to kill two birds with one stone, and squeeze in a game of cricket," Salmon told the press. He even attempted to explain, for the reporters' benefit, how the game is played. It was a lively contest. The star batter, who had paid extra to have all his best equipment flown in for the match, strode out to bat and was hit on the chest by the first ball he faced. The bowler appealed for leg before wicket. The umpire, who did not wish to spend too long in the early-winter cold, shot up his finger. "That's out! Let's not waste time here. It's too cold!"

Another batter hit the ball for six, right onto the middle of the Reykjavík ring road. A local bus had to be stopped so that it could be retrieved, much to the puzzlement of the passengers. It was an interesting game for the press. Or at least, it should have been.

> Cricket matches are very long, and their greatest intrigue is wondering why people bother to watch it at all. This was apparently a short game, lasting 'only' four hours.
>
> *Morgunblaðið*, 20 October 1979

31

Their lack of enthusiasm betrayed the national tendency to feel superior, even in a country still largely at a loss for recreation. During the pre-digital age, the nation's remoteness (and haughtiness) meant that any development in culture or media came late, or not at all. The currency was weak, and imports were prohibitively expensive, as was overseas travel. There was only one radio station until 1983, and it was limited to panel discussions and classical music. The solitary television channel came off air for the whole of July and didn't broadcast on Thursdays at all until 1987. Beer was illegal until 1989. Most of the roads were still gravel tracks. Inbound tourism was rare, and immigration close to zero.

The nineties in Iceland may as well have been the sixties anywhere else (the early sixties, that is, before anything got interesting). If you wanted to get away from the boredom, you saved up for a flight and went on a week-long binge in the Mediterranean: football, drinking, music and sex, and in that order.

Before 2000, fewer than five percent of Icelanders had satellite television. Those who did wanted to watch football. Icelanders have a particular affection for football clubs in northern English towns – Liverpool, Sunderland, Hull – where their fathers had emigrated to work in shipbuilding or fishing. Once the set-top box came along, they could at last watch their favourite teams from the comfortable sofa of a rich relative. Even then, Icelandic satellite television stopped short of screening whole games. The only reliable source of action was Sky Sports News, which then, as now, frequently interrupted the football to show adverts and – still more annoyingly – other sports.

Thus Icelandic football fans were fleetingly exposed to things of which they had no prior knowledge or experience. Lengthy and repetitive overtures to Fruit 'n' Fibre, the Abbey National building society and PG Tips segued into meandering, subdued footage of obese men throwing pointed cocktail sticks into a round coloured board, emaciated pensioners tiptoeing around a green carpet following a ball that wouldn't roll straight, and tall men dressed in white milkmen's suits alternately throwing a ball away from themselves as fast as they could, then chasing to get it back again.

It was this latter image that piqued the interest of 23-year-old Ragnar Kristinsson, a history graduate living in his uncle's apartment while he saved up to rent his own place. It was the autumn of 1996 and, as ever, there was little to do in the eastern suburbs of Reykjavík, just as there was little to do anywhere else in Iceland. Ragnar whiled away the long winter evenings watching football on satellite television. And during the breaks, those men in white milkmen's suits would be shown for a few moments.

In all probability, had Ragnar's friends and relatives known the seed of obsession that was planted, that winter, in his brain, they'd have called for the other men in white suits – the ones from Kleppur, the secluded psychiatric hospital in the woods near the harbour. Few Icelanders would have considered the game worthy of remark, let alone study. But then, Ragnar is not like other Icelanders.

III

RAGNAR

They should make a statue of Ragnar and put it outside the
Parliament building. People should walk out of Parliament and
be able to see a statue of Ragnar. On a horse.

Stebbi Ásmundsson, 2019

I first meet Ragnar in the lounge of the Natura Hotel, on the
slopes of Öskjuhlíð. The location could not be more appropriate:
the Natura was built on the site of the old Nissen huts where the
British forces whiled away their time during the war – where they
hatched the plan for the country's first modern cricket match.
There is no better place to become acquainted with the godfather
of 'krikket'.

Even his name seems apt. The name 'Ragnar' originally appeared
in the fifth century, scrawled on a wall in Carthage, which means
it's not only older than cricket, but older than Iceland itself. 'Ragnar'
translates as 'the Great Judge', which strikes me as a fitting tribute to
the man who brought cricket back home.

He looks like an Icelander, too. Tall and slouching, with broad
shoulders and a beer gut I bet he didn't have in his twenties. Apart
from a smart city overcoat of grey tweed, he looks every bit a
trawlerman: close-cropped greying hair, silver stubble, a weather-
worn complexion and bright, mischievous eyes. He speaks quietly,
with the distinctive Icelandic accent: round o's, rolled r's, and a
storyteller's lilt. He has a way of smirking as he tells his tale, as
though a wry aside or humorous twist is just around the corner –
which it usually is.

"I remember when I first saw cricket," he says. "It was on Sky
Sport News, when I was living with my uncle, after graduating.
I never understood any of it." He pauses, and gazes into the middle
distance. A degree of bafflement exists even now, more than two
decades later.

"You see rugby for the first time, and you see this team going this way, and that team going that way, and that's how they score. It's not difficult to work out. But this was completely different. You would see the scores: 406 and 204 for 6. You didn't even know who was winning. And I thought, what is going on? Does *anyone* win?"

Given that this was about the time of the infamous Test match that saw England and Zimbabwe scrap for five days in Bulawayo, only to draw with the scores level, you could forgive Ragnar for deciding the answer was "no". It is easy to forget what a closed book cricket can be to the newcomer, and it's obvious that – despite his pivotal role in the growth of Icelandic cricket – Ragnar still feels like an outsider.

"I just *had* to know what it was all about," he admits. "It became a fixation. Icelandic encyclopedias made no mention of it. And there was no internet video. But we'd recently got email. And I had a friend from university, Stebbi Ásmundsson, who was in Sussex doing a Master's degree in international law. Specialising in fishing rights."

No surprise there.

"So I emailed Stebbi and said, can he ask the English students about it? Or maybe find a game or something? He thought I was mad, of course, but he promised to try."

And so, as the rest of the cricket world gorged on the six-match banquet that was the 1997 Ashes, Ragnar was holed up in his uncle's apartment, piecing together evidence. One can imagine him, poring over a pinboard – the midnight sun illuminating it through the gaps in the window blinds – using lengths of string to link cricket reports transcribed from Sky, print-outs of dispatches from Stebbi and snippets from the *Encyclopedia Britannica*, parsed specifically and solely for the cricket references (and, let's be honest, we've all done that, haven't we?).

Ragnar eventually found a place of his own, but not in Reykjavík. He accepted a post as a teacher in the Vestmannaeyjar, a volcanic archipelago off the south coast, which had one small town and one tiny school. The job came with accommodation, and the accommodation came with Sky, permitting Ragnar to indulge his obsession further. Which was just as well, since there was almost nothing else to do on the island. There was only sport. Despite a population of just a few thousand, the island was a hotbed of sport.

The football club, Vestmannaeyjar FC – presumably having found a cure for seasickness – now managed to visit the mainland often enough to establish winning ways and did the Icelandic league and cup double in 1997 and 1998. The island also boasted a top-flight handball team.

Ragnar was a decent handball goalie, and it didn't take him long to get noticed. He'd thrown himself into school life, and frequently helped out with the physical education lessons. The island's handball team had been doing well, rising through the first division, and Ragnar was invited to train with them; he soon became the reserve goalkeeper. His big break came in the winter of 1998–99, when the team was pushing for its first title. The senior goalie fell ill, and Ragnar was selected to replace him. It was a crunch match – and would be televised. This was Ragnar's moment. He was on the verge of becoming the hero of the island; perform well, and he might even push for national honours.

Fate dealt a cruel blow. The day before the game, Ragnar was helping out at his school's sports day, and decided to join in a tug-of-war against his pupils. He won – but dislocated his shoulder while celebrating, and never played handball again. His dreams were dashed in an instant. I ask Ragnar how he felt.

"Not too bad, all things considered," he replies. "I mean, I *won* the tug of war."

And he still had a house, a good job, a decent income, and long holidays. In 1999, his school's summer vacation coincided with the conclusion of Stebbi's studies in Sussex, so they decided to go and turn themselves pink – Icelandic skin *never* tans – in Cyprus.

Icelanders love the Mediterranean. Whatever the time of year, the temperature is guaranteed to be warmer than any summer day in Iceland, you can linger on the beach without risking hypothermia, and the alcohol is cheap. Ragnar and Stebbi met in London where, passing time, they ambled into a betting shop – a novelty, since there was nothing of the kind back home. The television screens were showing cricket: the 1999 World Cup, no less. Ragnar decided that the first flutter of his life should be a cricketing one. He didn't know who the strong teams were, but he knew well enough not to back the favourite or rank outsider, so he picked Australia at 5–1 and threw down a few pounds.

And so to the Med. The modus operandi for an Icelander on holiday isn't complex. Sleep in, late breakfast, coffee, sit on the beach until you get too hot (which takes between seven and twelve minutes). Bar, beers, beef, beers, bed. Roman ruins and geological wonders tend to go unobserved.

Somewhere in Limassol, Ragnar and Stebbi found a 'British pub' which, to Ragnar's undisguised delight, was showing a World Cup match on a big screen. And – at last – there were English people around to explain it.

"It was the first time I had actually *watched* a game, rather than just seeing a report," recalls Ragnar. "And we were thinking, this is quite fun. It was entertaining. It was even exciting."

He recalls being mesmerised by the array of on-screen statistics while Steve Waugh was batting. The Australian captain was chasing a target and falling behind the required run-rate.

"We were saying, 'he should try more!' but he was going far too slowly. Then Stebbi got bored and wanted to go get a steak, so we left the pub, and I don't know what even happened in the end."

It was the Edgbaston semi-final – one of the most famous finishes in cricket history. And Ragnar's only memory was that the Australian captain batted too slowly.

The following Sunday, Ragnar and Stebbi were back in London, enjoying a lunchtime drink in Piccadilly. The bar had a television, and it was showing the final, being played up the road at Lord's. Entranced by the occasion, Ragnar suggested they find a pub near the ground, and drink there, to soak up the atmosphere. It was a bright and fair day, and children were playing cricket in Green Park as the Icelanders made their way to the tube. But by the time they'd reached St John's Wood, they found themselves among throngs of disheartened, departing Pakistan supporters. Australia, said the disappointed fans, were cruising to victory; the match was nearly gone. They thrust their match tickets into Ragnar's hands.

Ragnar was more bemused than delighted. His first cricket match in the flesh, and it was the World Cup final at Lord's. Not many people could boast that.

"It wasn't a huge deal," he shrugs. "It was just like a big stadium. I had only known for two days that there was even a place called Lord's, so it wasn't as if it was some kind of holy shrine. But it was filled up to the brim, and someone gave me a piece of paper with a 4 and a 6 on it, and we watched the last part of the match. Actually, we were part of the crowd that invaded the pitch at the end."

On returning to Piccadilly, Ragnar insisted on a visit to Lillywhite's in the hope of buying some cricket gear. Low on funds at the end of the boozy vacation, he picked out a pale-white Slazenger bat, which came in a starter kit with a set of stumps, bails and a red ball – the cheapest equipment he could find, on special offer for £10. And bearing his treasure, like Raleigh with his potato, or Joseph Smith with his golden plates, he returned triumphantly home.

The night is drawing in at the Natura Hotel. Ragnar and I have been talking – well, Ragnar has been talking and I have been listening – for the best part of three hours, and we both have work in the morning. Ragnar suggests we meet again, at a football match the following month. There, he assures me, he will introduce me to many of the people who helped him establish cricket in Iceland. I agree to come along, and Ragnar promises to send me details in due course.

It turns out that the football match is in England. Ragnar and his friends are as keen on English league football as everyone else in Iceland. I wonder which of the 'big three' shipbuilding clubs it will be. Liverpool? Sunderland? Hull? Ragnar informs me that it's a League One game in Luton.

"Oh, are Sunderland are playing away?" I ask. It seems a reasonable question, but Ragnar surprises me.

"No. Actually I support Luton."

"Why Luton?" I ask.

"Well, I just kind of chose them at random."

Ragnar is not like other Icelanders.

And so I wind up in Luton on a cold, grey Saturday morning in the middle of winter, nursing a watered-down Coke in a cavernous, dismal sports bar and waiting for Ragnar and his friends to appear. This is my chance to see how much of Ragnar's story is true, and which anecdotes this loquacious storyteller has embellished. When they arrive, my immediate thought is "Jesus. There are loads of them!", as if I didn't expect this many people to show up for a home game at Kenilworth Road, let alone travel a thousand miles to do it. I'd expected Ragnar to be accompanied by a few of his friends, not *all* of them. But there are at least twenty here, including half a dozen who were present at the rebirth of Icelandic cricket.

Stebbi is the first to be introduced. He is short and rotund, with tiny spectacles perched on a face of pinkest hue – a sort of Icelandic Billy Bunter. He has already got a good sweat going, suggesting that the Bedfordshire winter is proving uncomfortably warm for a well-insulated man of the Arctic. I expect him to full of cheery nostalgia for his days of cricketing discovery in Cyprus – in fact, he is anything but. His responses are hurried and perfunctory, and he punctuates his speech with dismissive hand gestures. At first, I interpret this as shyness; the Icelanders can be so reluctant to open up, they seem almost offhand, as though keen to be swiftly away from a conversation they would gladly never have had in the first place. But Stebbi is not shy. He just doesn't like cricket, and never has.

"Ah," he begins, with a sweep of the hand. "It was really not that fun. The English tourists were very interested in the cricket, and so was Ragnar, but not me."

"You weren't curious about it?" I ask, a little surprised.

"Not really," he replies. "If there was a choice between bars, and one was showing the cricket, and the other wasn't, Ragnar would drag me to the bar showing the cricket."

"But didn't you get into it, once you'd watched for a bit?"

"To be honest, no. I really couldn't work out what was going on. I couldn't even tell who was in which team."

"And yet you ended up actually going to the final?"

Another sweep of the hand.

"Ah, Lord's. It didn't really do anything for me, to be honest with you. I wouldn't say there was anything very unusual or surprising there. I can't really say I was hooked. And I've never watched a cricket match since."

Bugger. This isn't how the story's supposed to go.

"Don't mind about him," says Ragnar, sensing my discomfort. "He has not had a good life. When he moved back to Iceland, he headed the national delegation to the International Whaling Commission for about ten years and was persona non grata all over the world."

"I didn't actually *kill* the whales! I was just the legal advisor!" Stebbi protests.

"Either way, you still had to travel the world with the whale-killers," Ragnar counters. "It's no wonder you didn't have the heart to love something as beautiful as cricket."

I try to steer Ragnar back to the chronology. When he returned from London, bargain-basement cricket kit in tow, who *did* take an interest, if not Stebbi? Ragnar needs little encouragement to resume the story. The summer holidays of 1999, not yet over, brought another sporting occasion into prospect, this time in Laugarvatn. Though at first glance a small and nondescript village, next to a large and . nondescript lake, Laugarvatn is to Iceland what Loughborough is to England – sport's 'centre of excellence', where young and talented teenagers grow into sporting superstars. Ragnar, back at home on his tiny island, got a call from an old university friend, Stefán Pálsson. They'd studied history together, they hadn't seen each other for a while, and did Ragnar play football at all? Ragnar did. Stefán was playing in a late-August tournament at Laugarvatn, and his team were a player short. Could Ragnar make up the numbers? Ragnar could.

Ragnar introduces me to Stefán – who is also a Luton fan – as a "celebrity historian and national treasure," which suggests that he is likely to be talkative, and by God he is. He is a little Hobbit-like, with a mass of curly hair and beard, and tiny porcine eyes blinking through thick, black-rimmed spectacles. He looks like he has either just got out of bed, or not got into it for several days. There are still a couple of hours before kick-off, and Stefán is confident that, if I can keep the beers coming, he can guide me through at least the rest of 1999 and 2000 in that time. I ask him about the football team he was organising – and am immediately brought up on the importance of accuracy.

"Well, you know, that is not quite correct," says Stefán, with a historian's pedantry. "I was not actually organising the team. I just asked Ragnar to play. Valur organised the team." He shouts across the room. "Valur, *komdu hér!*"

A dapper, Luton-supporting man with smart spectacles and stubble turns from the bar. With his designer coat and scarf, he looks a little too well-turned-out for Luton. Valur Gunnlaugsson is very much the Norseman; his Scandinavian good looks could easily have got him into a wall calendar of Aryan pin-ups from the

1930s. Apart from being blond and blue-eyed, he is a dead ringer for Jürgen Klopp. The two men form a remarkable double-act: Stefán asking the questions, to which Valur can't remember the answers, but Stefán can.

"Do you remember where you met Ragnar?" is Stefán's starter for ten.

"Err … no," replies Valur.

"It was at the football tournament at Laugarvatn."

"Oh, okay."

"Do you remember your team was short of players?"

"No."

"It was short of players."

"Oh."

"Do you remember who I asked to come along?"

"No."

"Ragnar."

"Okay."

I ask why the football tournament is relevant.

"Well, Ragnar came along," says Stefán. "And he was, you know, telling everybody about cricket. At one stage he gave a practical demonstration to Benedikt." He gestures in the direction of another unmistakable Nordic.

Benedikt Waage is seriously Scandinavian, with the lightest flaxen hair and the palest skin, as though hewn from alabaster. He looks like he has just been released from cryogenic suspension. His appearance belies his warmth, for he has a chirpy, amused, almost puckish demeanour, and laughs irresistibly as he speaks, as though he is on the verge of a nervous giggle. He supports Luton.

"Ha, yeah. We had to stand around between matches," says Benedikt. "And one time, during a break, he said 'If you like, I can demonstrate cricket to you guys.' And I assumed he was joking. So I said, 'Ha, yeah, and if the lake freezes, I can demonstrate curling.' Nobody thought even for one minute he actually meant it. We would just sit on the grass and listen to Ragnar talking. Non-stop. Like it was a stand-up routine. He was telling us about how he used to play handball, or something."

"Yes, and do you remember what happened to him?" asks Stefán.

"No." Valur again.

"Ha, yeah. I think he told us a story," says Benedikt. "About how he was the reserve goalkeeper, and he was going to get some big break on television—"

"Yes, but I *won* the tug of war!"

Ragnar is with us again.

The tale unfolds. Ragnar returned to Reykjavík with the three footballing friends, and – deciding he'd spent enough time on the island – took a job with the insurance company Tryggingamiðstöðin ('The Insurance Company'). Every weekend, they would drag their cricket set – and Stebbi – down to Elliðaárdalur, a beautiful tree-fringed meadow with splashing streams and wild rabbits, to have a hit. Stefán, at that time a historian but not yet a celebrity one, ran the Museum of Electricity adjacent to the meadow, and they stored their equipment there.

When the winter came, Ragnar felt they should devise plans for something more concrete. All amateur cricketers will be familiar with the 'planning for greatness' that takes place in winter: the dream team is selected, the prestige event devised, the club tour planned. By the time the summer comes, there's no way it can possibly live up to the expectations the off-season has created. Ragnar's group weren't sure what their 'something concrete' should be, but felt they ought to be planning for it all the same.

The first step, they agreed, was to translate the laws of cricket into Icelandic. Since they were all working full-time, they enlisted a mutual acquaintance named Siggi Jónsson. He was "doing something involving computers" for the Reykjavík city council, preparing the municipality for the millennium bug, and since his team had pretty much worked out that there *was* no millennium bug, he had a lot of time on his hands (doing as little work as possible, until someone notices, is a strong contender for the title of Iceland's favourite pastime).

The imposing figure of Siggi – giant, bald, rugged and whiskered – raises his glass to me from the other side of the room. He cuts a statuesque figure, and speaks with a commanding, donnish authority. He is wearing the traditional Icelandic woollen sweater, the *lopapeysa*, the only member of the group self-assured enough to carry off the look. He resembles a headmaster leading a scouting expedition. Does he support Luton? Of course he does.

I ask him about the translation.

"Well, to begin with, it was very important not to use any *tökuorð*, of course," he says.

Icelanders, as the custodians of the original Norse, are determined never to permit the introduction of a 'taken word' – that is, one borrowed from another language – and are immensely protective of the Viking vernacular. Whenever something new comes along, the linguistic experts get together and decide on its Icelandic name; that is, what the Norse would have called it, if they'd had it back then. The famous example dates from 1965, when computers came along and the Icelanders couldn't tolerate the word 'komputer' because it would have made no sense to their ancestors. So they came up with *tölva*, meaning 'prophetess of numbers'.

Translating the modern cricketing lexicon into a vocabulary fit for a ninth century chieftain was quite a challenge, and one which Siggi threw himself into with considerable zeal, writing a 28-page pamphlet called *Krikketið Útskýrt* ('The Cricket Explained'), the purpose of which was to put the Icelandic *ingenu* in the picture. In anticipation of our meeting, he has brought along a copy. As I leaf through it, the others look over my shoulder.

"Hey, is that *Krikketið Útskýrt?*" asks Ragnar. "That's amazing! I haven't seen it for twenty years. Does it have all the Icelandic cricketing terms?"

"We were always emailing each other, you know, suggesting the best translations," says Stefán.

"Yeah, ha, sometimes we would spend an entire day on a single word," adds Benedikt.

"I don't remember this at all," murmurs Valur, glancing at the unfamiliar pages.

Stebbi remains silent. I have the impression the exercise was rather beneath him.

Krikketið Útskýrt is a work of genius. Nobody could accuse Siggi of shirking his duty to the mother tongue. Cricket has a language all its own, and somehow Siggi made that language Icelandic. Take his treatise, for example, on spin bowling. When you put his interpretation into Google, and translate it back into English, this is what you get:

Rectangular transplants can therefore be placed in two categories: reproof plots, which throw simple reprobes and protrusions; and grafting plaques, throwing breakthroughs, overshoots, liquid balls, and flippers. Fragments are one of the hardest to hit because it is impossible to see how every ball rotates. Breastfeeding, however, is less common than cessation because of the difficulty in perfecting the cast. Any other rotational naming system applies to left-handed porpoises.

Krikketið Útskýrt

Thanks to Siggi's assiduity, Icelandic students of the great summer game learned what agricultural strokeplay was (*Framsóknarslag* or 'like a member of the Farmers' Co-operative Party'), what it meant to bowl a maiden, or *að varpa heimasætunni á bakið* ('throw the cute farmgirl on her back'), and how to appeal in three different ways: *hvernig er 'ann* ('how is he'), *hvernig er'ða* ('howzat'), *hvernernn* ('howzee'). Some expressions were more literal, such as *leggjarframhjáhlaups* ('a run when the ball has glanced the leg').

Fielding positions posed the greatest problem, since many have abstruse names, and possibly also because Siggi believes he was drunk when they translated them. Wicketkeeper became 'warden of the gate', and third man became 'third wheel'. One term Siggi definitely got right was *fjölskyldudjásn*, the euphemistic 'crown jewels', to which he appended a note: 'this needs no further explanation.'

The sports bar is now starting to fill up with non-Icelandic Luton supporters, a species I'd started to suspect might not exist. It's getting a little loud, and since there's still an hour until kick-off, we stroll through the town and set up in a very different sort of pub. Squeezed amidst the terraced houses near Kenilworth Road, this place seems to have been borrowed from an industrial town of the north. The rooms are tiny and packed, crammed with big coats, stale with spilt ale and sweat. The Icelanders lay claim to the beer garden. No doubt they are the only ones who can bear the cold.

The conversations of Ragnar and my new acquaintances have turned from cricket to football. All except Stefán, who is now unstoppable. He wants to tell me about his television debut.

"You know, it is very strange to consider, since I have been on television so many times, that my first appearance was to discuss something I knew nothing about," he muses.

In a country where pretty much anything different is considered newsworthy – it's said that every Icelander appears on television at least three times in their life – the nascent cricket obsessives were considered a touch more eccentric than many others of their age. Ragnar was contacted by the producers of a daytime television show, *Silikon*, and invited to come and talk about cricket, live on air. He brought along the bat and ball and Stefán, to be interviewed by the show's presenter, a young, hip Icelandic model. Then they set up a practical demonstration.

"It was really ridiculous," Stefán recounts. "We knew pretty much zero about cricket, you know, and here we were, playing cricket in a tiny, bathroom-sized studio full of lights and cameras, for the benefit of the Icelandic nation."

There were immediate dividends. After the broadcast, a couple of students telephoned the studio asking how they could join in. Jóhannes Númason, a meat-slicer who fronted a rock band in his spare time, was keen. So was Ólafur Unnarsson, a milkman, apparently only notable for his nickname, 'Teflon', bestowed upon him by his friends, because he had once bought a sofa which bore the label 'contains Teflon'. He had been unable to shake off the moniker.

Now they were eight. Whiling away time in his insurance office and musing that his group was only three shy of constituting an actual team, Ragnar felt he now knew what the concrete plan should be: to form the national cricket team of Iceland. If they could get their numbers up to eleven, who could possibly say they *weren't* the national team? And who, then, could stop them from entering the next World Cup?

The Icelandic Cricket Association was founded on 14 August 1999, at a meeting attended by the eight 'originals': Ragnar, Stebbi, Stefán, Valur, Benedikt, Siggi, Jóhannes the meat-slicer and Teflon, plus a ninth, their friend Kári Ólafsson, who was just about to leave the city for a job in a coastal fish processing factory, and seven sundry others, who were presumably just there for the beer.

Stefán, buoyed by his first television appearance, scuttled about trying to talk to the media, while Benedikt browsed the web and found something called the European Cricket Council. He fired off a speculative email, attaching a heavily doctored digital photograph showing more players than they had, enjoying a game of cricket next to the Museum of Electricity, and enquiring if they would be interested in an Iceland team. Within a day or so, the Icelandic Cricket Association was listed on the ECC website, listing Ragnar as chairman, Benedikt as secretary and Stefán as press officer. They had still not played an actual match.

In the spring of 2000, Stebbi paid a visit to his old university friends in Sussex and, on returning to Iceland, went down to Elliðaárdalur to find Ragnar and the others practising. He bore a cricket ball and bad news. The cricket ball *was* the bad news. It was not like the ball that had come with the cricket set. It was a lot harder. A lot shinier. It had string stitched round it. Was Stebbi sure it was a proper cricket ball? Stebbi had been assured that it was. But a cricket ball is like a red tennis ball, isn't it? Stebbi shrugged. There was consternation. *This* is a real cricket ball? What do you do if it hits you?

Benedikt made a hasty call to the ECC. Yes, they confirmed, a cricket ball is shiny and hard and has stitching. No, not like a tennis ball. Yes, it hurts. No, players wear protecting clothing. Yes, they would send some.

Not long afterwards, a bag of cricket equipment arrived at the international airport, addressed to Benedikt, and with a hefty import tax payable. This is one of the annoyances of living in Iceland. Every parcel that arrives, and I mean *every* parcel, is valued and the recipient charged 24 per cent of that value, whatever it is. At that time, there was a loophole for wedding presents. Benedikt tried to claim that he and Ragnar were engaged, but because same-sex marriage wasn't to be legalised in Iceland for another ten years, the ruse failed.

When the bag was brought to Elliðaárdalur, the enthusiasts fell upon its contents with a mixture of glee and bewilderment. Everything was carefully shared out between the nine of them. There were a dozen hard cricket balls. There were three or four bats – much larger than the ICA's bat. It rapidly became clear that Ragnar and Stebbi had unwittingly bought a backyard cricket set for a small child, and that these strapping Icelandic men had been trying to get to grips with it for the best part of a year. Gloves, check.

Batting pads, check. Everybody quickly worked out what a box was for. They weren't *that* naive. There was only one piece of equipment that proved a total mystery, and they put it to the use they thought best, which is why the very earliest photographs of Icelandic cricket show batters kitted out in brand-new gear with thigh pads strapped to their stomachs.

Stefán begins again.

"So this call came through from a guy in England. He said he'd found our number on the ECC website. I believe he was a barrister in Manchester and he had a stag weekend booked in Iceland at the end of the summer. He had a cricket team called the Utopians, from Oxford, you know, and he wanted to play a match against the Iceland cricket team. And we didn't dare tell him, you know, that we had no cricket team at all, just nine people with a big bag of kit that we didn't know what to do with. So we said yes."

It was agreed that, before the Iceland national team – okay, they were still two short – attempted to play against a visiting team from England, there really ought to be a practice game: eleven against eleven, all Icelanders. For this, they needed to form *two* teams – and they didn't quite have *one* yet.

The bright idea came from Kári, newly arrived in the fishing village of Stykkishólmur, about 175 kilometres north of Reykjavík. He hadn't been there long, but the lads in the fish factory had invited him to get to know a few people by joining the local social club. Kári suggested that the men from the city could drive out to the village to play cricket against the locals; he quickly found eleven villagers who thought it sounded like fun.

Back in the capital, there was another stroke of luck. Two cricket-loving immigrants, Dharmendra Bohra and Sammy Gill, had recently come to Iceland and – thanks once more to the ECC website – had found that cricket was played there. Dharmendra was a stonemason from India, apparently a skill in short supply in Iceland. Sammy was a Christian missionary from Pakistan. His father was a professor at the Adventist college and seminary in Farooqabad; Sammy studied and played cricket there before moving to Reykjavík, where he sold religious books door-to-door, and settled down with an Icelandic woman. The two expats joined up just in time for the practice game. At last, Ragnar had his eleven.

Stefán says there was now just one missing piece of the jigsaw. "Well, you know, we figured if we are going to send a team out to Stykkishólmur to play the social club, our team needed a name. And we couldn't call ourselves Krikketklúbbur Reykjavíkur because that would have the same initials as Knattspyrnufélag Reykjavíkur [Reykjavík FC]. So we decided to call ourselves Kylfan Krikket Klúbbur Reykjavíkur, or 'Kylfan' for short".

I recall that *kylfan* means 'the bat', according to Siggi's translation.

"So there it was," shrugs Stefán. "Kylfan versus Stykkishólmur on the *Danskirdagar*."

Every village in Iceland has its own festival week, or *hátíð*. In Stykkishólmur, they celebrate the *Danskirdagar* (Danish Days), during which the villagers have numerous Danish-themed events. I ask Stefán what this involves.

"Oh, you know, they all dress up as the Danish queen and play with Lego or whatever. So we went up there and they'd tried to build a little airstrip for the village and it hadn't taken off, so to speak. There was a small deserted terminal building, so, you know, we slept there for the weekend. And some of us got very drunk."

I note that Stefán is the best part of five pints down already, and we're still ahead of kick-off.

"Yes, I was the most drunk. I was also the most hungover. So, you know, we decided I would be wicketkeeper, because we figured he doesn't move about very much. And, well, we got that wrong for a start."

The other thing that the Kylfan players got wrong was to underestimate their rural counterparts. A few weeks before the match, when Kári asked around the social club, he'd found himself eleven volunteers in just a few minutes. None of them had even seen cricket before, let alone held a cricket bat or ball, but why not? It was something to do. The two foreigners, Dharmendra and Sammy, hadn't yet had the chance to practise with their own team, who had themselves only knocked about in the meadows four or five times anyway. But while the Kylfan men drank themselves to sleep, the expats offered a few tips to the lads from the village. The guidance may have been basic, but it was remarkably effective.

Teflon, who worked at the national dairy, had arranged for all the players to wear white milkmen's clothing for the match (the dairy even provided a trophy for the winning team). Stykkishólmur batted first, and slowly amassed a modest total of 60 runs, mostly in wides. To Kylfan's great embarrassment, they could not overtake the novices' score.

Ragnar bullishly remarked that Kylfan may have been defeated in the league, but they would gain revenge in the cup. And now, with a chastened Dharmendra and Sammy in tow, he brought his team back to the city, where the two genuine cricketers gave their team-mates a good deal more instruction than they had bestowed upon the villagers. They learned to bowl rather than throw. They learned to nudge the ball for ones and twos rather than trying to hit it to the boundary every time.

Stefán recalls the rate of improvement.

"We went up again in August for a rematch, which we called the Icelandic Cricket Cup. Both teams had the same players as before, but we beat them heavily."

Photographs show Teflon receiving the player of the match award, though nobody can remember why he got it.

"We became quite pleased with ourselves," continues Stefán. "We had some t-shirts made bearing the team name, KKK Reykjavík, and then I went to the Edinburgh Festival, you know, wearing my t-shirt pretty much all the time. And I got pushed around everywhere I went. I got beaten up in the street at least twice. I had no idea why."

In anticipation of the arrival of the stag party from Manchester, it was agreed that the ICA ought to have some sort of official recognition at home. The Icelanders love bureaucracy in all its forms. Meetings, resolutions, papers – they live for it. Becoming an official sport takes years, sometimes even decades. The application criteria are onerous. It was quite an achievement even to be allowed a meeting with the bigwigs at the ÍSÍ, the Icelandic Sports Association. But Benedikt was granted a preliminary hearing, and dutifully sat there while the ÍSÍ representatives ran through the usual spiel: cricket has only been played here a couple of months, there is very little money to go round, come back in a few years perhaps, and we'll discuss how to begin the application process. They agreed, at least, to take Benedikt's name and contact details.

"Benedikt G. Waage," he began. The entire panel looked up. Pens suddenly dropped, mouths slowly opened, and eyes gradually lifted to the portrait hanging on the wall above the door. The founder of the ÍSÍ. The godfather of Icelandic sport. Benedikt turned to look and was astonished to be greeted with the likeness of his own great-grandfather. A gold plate beneath the painting bore the inscription:

BENEDIKT G. WAAGE

Ten minutes later, Benedikt emerged from the ÍSÍ building, bearing the Icelandic Cricket Association's official articles of recognition. Ragnar and his friends had been playing cricket for a combined total of about twelve hours.

HOW TO SPEAK CRICKET IN OLD NORSE

BATTING

bat	**kylfa** *club* (or **knatttré** *ball-tree*)
batter	**kylfill** *clubber*
striker	**sóknarkylfill** *club-attacker*
non-striker	**meðsóknarkylfill** *club-attacker's companion*
partner	**kylfilsfóstbróðir** *sworn brother with the club*
batting average	**meðalsláttur** *average reaping*
block	**hindrun** *hindrance*
French cut	**Danskkantur** *Danish edge*
agricultural stroke	**Framsóknarslag** *in the style of a member of the Farmers' Agricultural Party*

BOWLING

ball	**bolti** *ball* (or **knöttur** *knot*)
bowler	**verpill** *hurler*
fast bowler	**hraðverpill** *rapid-hurler*
spin bowler	**spunaverpill** *spin-hurler*
wicket	**vik** (abbr. of **brottvikning**) *dismissal*
bowling average	**meðalfórn** *average sacrifice*
yorker	**Jórvíkingur** *a Viking from York*

INFRASTRUCTURE

wicket | **vikket** (abbr. of **vikjas**) *wicket-gate*
bail | **snælda** *spindle*
pitch | **varpsvæði** *hurling-area* (also *nesting area*)
off-side | **úthlið** *windward side*
on-side | **landhlið** *leeward side*
floodlights | **töfralýsing** *magic lighting*

GAME PLAY

run | **hlaup** *leap*
over | **lok** *the end*
total | **stig** *points*
extra | **aukastig** *other points*
umpire | **dómari** *judge*
tea break | **kaffihlé** *coffee break*

FIELDING

fielder | **vallaleikmann** *field-player*
wicketkeeper | **vikketvörður** *warden of the gate*
first slip | **fyrsta skyssa** *first slip*
second slip | **önnur skyssa** *another slip*
third man | **þriðja hjólið** *third wheel*
deep | **djúpur** *deep*
silly | **bjálfi** *barmy*

DISMISSALS

bowled | **varpað út** *hurled out*
caught | **gripinn** *grasped*
hit wicket | **rakst í vikket** *wrecked the gate*
timed out | **fallinn á tíma** *ran out of time*

IDIOMS

bowl a maiden | **að varpa heimasætunni á bakið**
hurl the cute farmgirl on her back
duck | **straumönd** *river-duck*
golden duck | **valur** *falcon*
nightwatchman | **næturvörður** *night-warden*
back in the hutch | **köttinn í sekknum** *the*
cat's back in the sack
ferret | **mörður** *ferret*
crown jewels | **fjölskyldudjásn** *family jewels*
it went through him | **fór milli eyrnanna** *went between his ears*
tickle | **kitl** *tickle (of the non-flirtatous variety)*

Note: all these terms are used in modern Icelandic.

IV
BLUFFING

ICELAND BEATS ENGLAND AT CRICKET
Iceland beat England 107 to 94 in the first game of the Iceland
national cricket team at Tungubakkavellir in Mosfellsbær on
Saturday. The Icelandic team has two foreign players, both
married to Icelandic women. The game took about four hours,
but team spokesman Valur Gunnlaugsson says nobody got tired
because there is little effort involved in playing cricket. He says
the English team has made a firm offer to host the Iceland team
in Britain. The offer is quite tempting, because one of them has
invited our team to stay in his private castle in Scotland.

Morgunblaðið, 11 September 2000

The summer was fading fast, as it does near the Arctic Circle.
September brought the first chilly north-westerlies of winter, but
from the opposite direction, it brought the Utopians team and their
stag party.

"We genuinely didn't believe they were coming, you know," says
Stefán. "We thought it was a joke."

Kick-off is drawing near in Luton, and the tiny pub has started to
empty. Some of the Icelanders are keen to get to the ground, but
Stefán is in full flow.

"They were from Oxford," he continues. "And they were educated,
you know. Lawyers. They said to meet them at a restaurant. We
figured, they must be really respectable guys. So that was another
thing we were wrong about."

As we stroll towards the ground, Ragnar, Stefán and Benedikt
recall the night. It may have been nineteen years previously, but it
evidently formed what psychotherapists call a 'critical life experience'.

"Yeah, it was the three of us," says Ragnar. "And ten of them." One
of the stag party had misunderstood his instructions and flown to
Sweden by mistake.

"And, ha, this was a time when there were strip clubs in Reykjavík," adds Benedikt.

"Yes, the boom years, you know," agrees Stefán. "We would rarely go to those kinds of places," says Ragnar. "But at that time, all the bars had stopped serving alcohol at 3 a.m. so sometimes you would go to the strip club just to keep drinking, because they served all night."

"But, ha, these guys wanted to go to the strip clubs at, like, 10 p.m." adds Benedikt.

"So we went from one club to the next," Ragnar continues. "And every time we moved on, we left another one of the English guys behind."

Benedikt shakes his head.

"Yeah, ha, there was no way we could keep up with them," he says.

"So we decided to do shifts with them, you know," says Stefán. "And one of them said to me, 'do young gentlemen use recreational drugs here?'"

"And that was the first time I saw cocaine!" laughs Ragnar.

It was generally felt that there was no conceivable way the Utopians would be able to play cricket the following day. The Icelanders assumed the revellers wouldn't show up and would forfeit the game. But somehow, one by one, they all turned up ahead of time, at the Tungubakkavellir football fields in Mosfellsbær, about half an hour east of Reykjavík (Stykkishólmur had been deemed too distant for the fixture).

"They were, ha, really, really happy," recalls Benedikt.

"Well, of course they were," replies Ragnar. "They were still drunk. But by noon, they got a bit fresher. I think probably with some assistance."

All three remember the game as clearly as they recall the night that preceded it. Expecting a team of fairly clueless Icelanders, the Utopians took a relaxed approach to the game – and a more serious approach to their drinking – and were hit all over the park by Dharmendra and Sammy. The nine local players did their best for the press cameras.

"We phoned in the result to the newspaper and, without really thinking, we called the teams Iceland and England," says Ragnar. "And then came the headline: 'Iceland beats England at cricket.'"

"It just underlined how cricket was not considered a serious sport," agrees Stefán. "We were often covered in little amusing news features – you know, 'and *finally...*' – but never in the sports pages, where someone would probably have questioned our claims."

"So we invented clickbait as well," laughs Ragnar.

We arrive at the stadium and are instantly greeted by an announcement on the PA system: "We would like to welcome you all to Kenilworth Road today, especially the Iceland national cricket team, who are visiting for the weekend, and are all Luton supporters."

We are cheered to our seats, and Luton win 4–0.

One could be forgiven for thinking that, in little more than a year, Ragnar's dream had come to completion: the first cricket match between two teams comprised entirely of Icelanders, followed by a representative Iceland team beating an English team (or 'the' English team, depending on whether you read an Icelandic newspaper or not). There was every reason to believe the fun experiment was over – but a juggernaut had been started. Thanks to the ECC website, there was no let-up in enquiries from abroad.

I next meet Ragnar a couple of weeks later, at his local haunt: the Ölhúsið bar in Hafnarfjördur, a little to the south of Reykjavík. It is a cold, dank day and there is sleet about, but Ragnar is chipper as he picks up the tale. He recalls that 2001 brought three important phone calls from overseas, each more important than the last.

The first was from Matthew Engel, then editor of *Wisden Cricketers' Almanack*, who had recently introduced a new section called 'Cricket Round the World' and had noticed Iceland's recent emergence. Without knowing what *Wisden* was, Benedikt penned a brief article, and his name – and Ragnar's – duly appeared in print when the little yellow book arrived in April.

"There is, I think, a tradition that a club's worst player becomes the secretary," Ragnar suggests. I have been a club secretary and agree that he may have a point.

"Well," he continues, "it is absolutely the case that Benedikt and I are the worst players ever to have their names in *Wisden*. We were the only two Icelandic players to be mentioned, and we were the worst cricketers out of everyone. Well, actually, I could bowl a bit, so that makes Benedikt the worst. He was really dreadful."

Nevertheless, there they were, in black and write, at the top of page 1447. Incidentally, on page 954 of the same edition was the seemingly unrelated entry: N. L. Williams, three matches for Essex 2nd XI, 54 runs, highest score 48, four wickets, best bowling 3 for 8. Its relevance would become clear several years later.

Next on the phone was the ECC.

"They asked me to come to London to meet with them," says Ragnar. "So I went, and I brought them a bottle of *brennivín*, and they proudly gave me a tour of Lord's. I didn't have the heart to tell them I had already been."

The administrators were enthusiastic, to say the least. Even as the Icelanders' own interest in cricket waned – they'd had their fun – the ECC were now irrepressible.

"It was hopeless," sighs Ragnar. "They just would not go away. In 2001, we weren't really active. Maybe we had a knockabout once or twice in Elliðaárdalur, but they kept asking us if we wanted them to send us a coach. We said no, we were fine as we were, but they wouldn't give up. So in the end we caved in, and said okay."

In short order, the ECC had packed an experienced coach, Tim Dellor, off to Iceland.

Ragnar flinches with embarrassment at the memory.

"I took him to my place and stuck him in a spare room on a mattress. We'd told the ECC we had cricket practices every week in a sports hall, but in reality we had no cricket going on at all, and we'd never set foot in a sports hall. We just had no idea what to do with him."

That night, Ragnar anxiously called Stefán and Benedikt, who called all the other cricketers in the city, but to no avail. Stebbi was visiting his old university friends in Sussex, Valur, Siggi and Teflon were on holiday, Jóhannes the meat-slicer was at a slaughterhouse, and Dharmendra and Sammy were with their families overseas.

In desperation, Ragnar called Kári at the social club in Stykkishólmur.

"You're in luck," came the reply. "The boys' football team has a practice on Sunday. Come on up. It'll be fun."

A couple of days later, Dellor found himself being driven by Ragnar to "our weekly practice" which apparently involved a

350-kilometre round trip to a fishing village. Here he would coach a bunch of junior players who had, in reality, never heard of cricket before. Oh, and he would be spending the night in a sleeping bag by the airstrip.

Ragnar recalls how, on arrival in the village, Dellor showed him a copy of *The Times* announcing, with great sincerity, the auspicious occasion of his visit.

THE APPEAL OF CRICKET SPREADS TO ICELAND

On Sunday 20 May, 25 countries will participate in European Cricket Day, an event designed to raise the profile of the game in places as diverse as Ukraine, Finland, Estonia and Portugal. But perhaps the most ambitious task will be undertaken by Tim Dellor, in presenting a cricket course in Stykkishólmur, a town in Iceland to the north-west of Reykjavík. It is the most northerly registered outpost of the sport in the world.

The Times, 18 May 2001

By all accounts, it went well. Ragnar remembers Dellor was impressed – and so, incidentally, does Dellor.

"They weren't all that bad," he later told me. "What really impressed me was the athletic level of the Icelandic kids. I thought they were a lot more physically advanced and co-ordinated than children in the UK."

Dellor did not detect the deception; even when we spoke, I couldn't summon the courage to tell him.

"We really thought we had got away with it," says Ragnar, ruefully.

The third phone call came in early July. It was from an English woman who'd read the article in *The Times* and wanted to ask about Icelandic cricket. Ragnar had become used to this sort of conversation – there were frequent calls from cricket obsessives abroad – and he gave her the usual patter about how active and popular the sport was in Iceland.

The woman asked when the next match would be. Ragnar was loath to disappoint her.

"Oh, well, actually it's the Icelandic Cricket Cup final this weekend," he lied.

"That's great!" replied the woman. "We'll send a crew over to cover it."

"A crew? Who did you say you are?"

"Oh, sorry. I thought I told you. I'm from Sky Sports News."

Ragnar looks into his beer glass. It's the first time I've seen him looking a little bashful.

"Just for a moment, I felt I should admit I had lied," he says. "But I thought about it a little longer."

He looks up at me, impishly.

"And I thought, to hell with it. Why not?"

And so, for a second time that year, Ragnar had to get his players together to act out a face-saving charade, just as they had done with Dellor. The only trouble was, he'd only had to stage a cricket practice session for Dellor. For Sky, he needed to put together a full-scale cup final.

Fortunately, a handful of the Kylfan players who'd hosted the Utopians were prepared to engage in the pretence – but this time, the call to Kári in Stykkishólmur was less positive. Several of the social club men were at sea, and there was no way any of Dellor's young pupils could make it all the way to Reykjavík. When all the reckoning was done, Ragnar had six Kylfan players: himself, Benedikt, Jóhannes the meat-slicer, a very reluctant Stebbi, and the two genuine cricketers, Dharmendra and Sammy. Five men were willing to travel from the social club in Stykkishólmur. But that still left him a whole team short. Most Icelanders would have made a shame-faced call to Sky, scratching the game.

But Ragnar is not like other Icelanders. By now he'd made many friends at Tryggingamiðstöðin, and one by one, he added more players – the majority more amused than enthusiastic – to his roster. If they had just one training session, a couple of hours before the television crew turned up, they might be able to wing it. Ragnar's bosses, convinced that their hitherto unknown insurance company was now on the cusp of international fame, bought white polo shirts for their team. The dairy sent over a few more milkmen's uniforms. When cup final day came along, everyone *looked* like cricketers – as long as they didn't move about too much.

SKY TO COVER TODAY'S ICELANDIC CRICKET CUP

The Icelandic Cricket Cup will be held at Tungubakkavellir in Mosfellsbær today. Journalists from the British television station Sky Sports have come here to report from the match. Ragnar Kristinsson, the Chairman of the Icelandic Cricket Association, says he cannot imagine what is causing this interest in cricket in Iceland. He says the staff of the European Cricket Council have told him that queries about cricket in Iceland account for the vast majority of all the requests the Council receives. "They are amazed that you can play cricket here," says Ragnar. "I really do not know if we should tell them that there is hardly any cricket in Iceland. It's all a big misunderstanding."

Morgunblaðið, 28 July 2001

At Tungubakkavellir, the insurance brokers were hastily dressed as milkmen, shown how to put on their pads and which end of the bat to hold, and given lightning-quick instruction by Dharmendra and Sammy. The Sky people arrived, and the 'cup final' was played, with careful stage management to ensure that the novices were not exposed to the camera's scrutiny.

To everyone's relief – and to the delight of the television crew – Dharmendra and Sammy made big scores against the wayward bowling and hapless fielding. Kylfan made 111 and bowled Tryggingamiðstöðin out for 53, whereupon pictures of Ragnar lifting the Icelandic Cricket Cup were shown around the world – and all over Iceland, too, since every television station and newspaper sent reporters to report, if not the game itself, the news that Sky was covering it.

"Everyone wrote about it," Ragnar recalls. "And every single interviewer came completely from the mountains [an Icelandic saying that means someone knows absolutely nothing about something]. In one weekend, we got more coverage than most European cricketing nations have ever had."

He exhales deeply.

"It was exhausting. Not just the match, but Sky wanted to film at the Blue Lagoon, the hot springs, and all the landmarks in Reykjavík; it was a whole feature about Iceland. And we never received any recognition from the Icelandic tourist board. Nothing."

It is clear that Ragnar is proud and embarrassed in equal measure.

"Well, you see, we were just lying through our teeth," he admits. "But there was so much interest from other countries, I just didn't want to disappoint people."

I suggest he was also motivated by a mischievous impulse to see just how much he could get away with.

"Yes – that as well."

The deceptions of 2001 have endured. Indeed, the truth has been concealed until now. Even *Wisden*, in its next edition, proffered the official versions of Dellor's visit and the cup final that wasn't. It almost seems like heresy to have deceived the likes of Sky, *The Times*, and cricket's bible. Nevertheless, these sorties into cricketing battle seem to have sustained local appetite for the game over the next couple of years.

Ragnar tells me he thinks there was a third Icelandic Cricket Cup match in 2002, but he can't say for sure. I reach into my bag and produce a newspaper report of the game, an action photograph and – with a flourish – the original scoresheet. Ragnar stares at the photograph with a combination of nostalgia and amusement. The backdrop is the Víðistaðatún, a small park in Hafnarfjörður, set in a natural amphitheatre, overlooked by an attractive modernist church. The turf is beautifully green. It is an impressive setting – a huge improvement from the nondescript football fields at Tungubakkavellir. In the foreground, Jóhannes the meat-slicer is cutting the ball uppishly towards cover, where it will be caught.

"We made sure we always dressed right," says Ragnar. "All in white, wearing – well – suits, we thought."

He reminds me that, for many, the attire was the highlight of the day.

"We always drank tea at the tea interval. And we were very, very well behaved."

I ask Ragnar what he means by "well behaved". Icelanders are usually very competitive at sport. They're dignified losers but, accustomed to being underdogs, they don't half gloat if they win.

"Well, we'd formed this belief that cricket was so polite and genteel that you would never, ever approach the umpire like footballers do with the referee. If we thought someone was out, and they didn't go, we just kept quiet. We wouldn't ask the umpire 'how's that?' because we thought that wasn't the done thing, tantamount to cheating. And we were genuinely disappointed when we later discovered that wasn't the case."

No doubt the participation of more cricketing expats helped disabuse the locals of this quaint notion. The teams now boasted two Englishmen, two Indians, a South African and a Pakistani. Tryggingamiðstöðin avenged the previous year's defeat by racking up 172, the highest total yet made in Iceland; Sammy made 78, the first Icelandic half-century since Surgeon-Lieutenant Rice. Even Benedikt made 8, which turned out to be the highest score of his cricketing life. Despite a strong all-round performance from Dharmendra, Kylfan couldn't get close.

Ragnar admits that the prowess of the expats lent the team momentum.

"It was proving quite addictive," he concedes. "I mean, originally our aim was quite simple: to have a match with 22 players in neat white suits, drinking tea and being polite to each other. Then the idea came to have the Iceland national team. Every time we ticked off one of these aims, someone else came up with a new idea. And each time, lots of people wanted to play. So it sort of kept going, like it had a force all of its own."

It was about this time that Icelandic investors were busy throwing money into companies all over the world. From the Hamleys toy brand, to West Ham Football Club; you name it, there were probably *krónur* in it. We all know what was to come of that, but before the bubble burst, there was quite a boom.

One of the larger scale ventures was the launch of a low-cost airline called Iceland Express, established as a competitor to the national carrier, Icelandair. Unlike its rather staid rival, Iceland Express was showy and cheap. It was set to serve 17 international destinations each week, albeit with only two planes. With the first flights scheduled for 2003, the airline needed a big opening event to grab public attention. Somewhat bizarrely, the company decided to stage a celebrity cricket match in Iceland.

It wasn't a speculative move, either; it was a big, all-guns-blazing operation. The Iceland Express people told Ragnar that EFG, a private bank, would assemble a team – the Effigies – from its offices all over the world. They wanted to play one match under the midnight sun, and another on a glacier. They wanted a reception with the British ambassador. The team would be captained by the director of the bank and accompanied by Tim Dellor as coach and Henry Blofeld (a star of the BBC's cricket coverage) as commentator. Oh, and Bruce Dickinson – the lead singer of Iron Maiden – would be flying the plane.

Ragnar could have been forgiven for taking all this with a pinch of salt, but after Dellor's previous impromptu trip, not to mention the visit from Sky, he had learned not to count on bluff. Enlisting the support of the ambassador's vice-consul, a cricket obsessive named Simon Minshull, he mustered his players for earnest practice, back where it all began, among the rabbits and streams of Elliðaárdalur. This time, they had adult-sized bats and – if you will – adult-sized balls.

The Iceland Express publicity machine went into overdrive. A national newspaper was despatched to take photographs of the training sessions, and wrote three previews of the match, in the weeks that preceded it. Ragnar and Benedikt were conscripted to appear on *Kastljós*, Iceland's prime-time television talk show, to speak about the game. Their interviewer was Sigmundur Davíð Gunnlaugsson, who would later become Prime Minister.

Iceland's banks, still some years from their downfall, were spending money like water, and made no exception for the Icelandic cricketers. Keen to impress EFG, they had proper cable-knit cricket sweaters made for the team, and organised marquees and dainty teas. The Icelandic Equestrian Association supplied white trousers.

And then, spectacularly, the Iceland Express Boeing 737 touched down in Reykjavík as Iron Maiden's *Flight of Icarus* blasted from the PA system. The evening sun shone, the bankers disembarked like rock stars – as did the rock star himself – and the circus descended on the national sports stadium at Laugardalur. The bankers had brought not only a cricket scoreboard but also an artificial pitch, which was hastily installed.

At quarter to midnight, the match began. Blofeld, the most recognisable voice in cricket broadcasting, had a glass of red wine pressed into his hand and was pushed towards the middle as umpire. He had few opportunities to drink, as Dickinson's first over included eighteen wides. For the first time, Icelandic cricket had plenty of spectators: dozens of long-haired teenagers in Iron Maiden shirts jostled for autographs and handshakes. The alcohol flowed in ever-increasing volumes, and while the bankers caroused, the bemused Icelanders – batting on a flat pitch for the first time in their lives – ran up a big score. They still lost, of course.

Ragnar recalls one detail with particular relish.

"It was the bowling of Bruce Dickinson," he says. "It made us all realise how much we had learned as cricketers. I mean, he was way worse than any of us."

Though the match finished in the small hours, the bankers were in no mood to retire. They went straight from the stadium to the city's fleshpots; their captain performed the dance from *Rocky* on the podium at the Nasa Club.

"We were just thinking, what in God's name is that man doing?" recalls Ragnar. "But then again, what were *any* of us doing? It was like being in some weird hallucination."

The following day's game was the showpiece fixture – a daytime game. The bankers, somehow, had recovered from the night's exertions, and proved to be bullish with the bat. Even with five batters retiring, they knocked up 183, a new record score in Iceland; Dellor diplomatically delayed his own appearance until the last moment, but still hit a swift, unbeaten 17. The vice-consul, in front of his ambassador, took a good catch, but broke a finger in the process. Sammy's half-century, the first for anyone representing the national team, was not enough to bring the hosts victory.

The Langjökull glacier is a vast ice cap, covering about half the area of London. Beset by high winds and blizzards, it is impossible to walk across; in the high summer, a tour company takes visitors a little way up to inspect the ice, but it is far from hospitable. In early 2020, three dozen tourists were stranded there overnight, alongside their foolhardy and embarrassed local guides. It is perhaps the most unusual place ever to have staged a cricket match. The day after they beat Iceland, the Effigies and their entourage were swaddled in snowsuits, stuffed into a sno-cat, and hauled up the glacier. As the wind howled, it was hard enough to hold the pitch down, let alone bat on it, but the bankers did their best to play amid the driving snow and low cloud. They had brought half a dozen fluorescent yellow balls; once all were lost (which took about fifteen minutes), play came to a halt. The local press loved it, and Iceland Express got the publicity it craved – in Iceland, at least.

From the glacier, the bankers travelled west. Dellor had been intimately involved in the planning of the tour and was insistent that a visit should be made to the 'children's cricket academy' he'd seen in action in Stykkishólmur two years previously. The Effigies, he suggested, could take on the juniors; this was just the sort of thing touring teams should do.

It was late in the evening by the time the touring party, slowly thawing, reached the relative warmth of the village. The locals batted first, and made 109, with a local fish-portioning expert scoring 38. The visitors reached the target at two o'clock in the morning. Thus the Effigies, not to mention Iceland Express, completed their sub-Arctic sojourn well pleased; the Icelanders, on the other hand, found the whole occasion somewhat sobering. Were they becoming stooges for someone else's joke?

"I think most of the guys stopped playing after that tour," concludes Ragnar. "The midnight match, the guy from Iron Maiden, the glacier cricket, you know, it all felt a bit silly, frankly. I know Stefán thought it stopped being funny at that point. People started drifting away, having kids, finding other hobbies and so on. So we thought, let's have one more match at the end of the season. Kylfan against Stykkishólmur, just like how it started."

Ragnar called the troops together one last time, and they made the trip to Stykkishólmur for a final hurrah. This swansong, the fourth of the original Icelandic Cricket Cup matches, featured a young Icelandic actress called Ásta Sól Kristjánsdóttir, who became the first woman to play cricket in Iceland, making a duck for Kylfan and taking two wickets in the inevitable Stykkishólmur collapse. As the match came to a conclusion, she was struck in the face by the ball and sustained such terrible bruises that, the following week, her concerned neighbours called the police, who put a number of awkward questions to her boyfriend. Since he had also been playing in the match, he had a ready answer, but this necessitated a detailed explanation of the game of cricket to the increasingly confused officers of the law, who had never heard of it.

The match – and the injury – only served to reinforce the general view that it was time to draw the line under the cricketing adventures. Ragnar had only been able to muster three Icelandic players (including Ásta Sól) for the city team. And though Kári had again assembled a full eleven for the village, they'd been 15 for 6 after 12 overs, for heaven's sake – and all 15 of those runs had been extras. It was widely felt that continuing to play cricket was akin to flogging a dead horse.

The ICA still existed, with Ragnar as chairman, Benedikt as secretary and Sammy as senior player, even after the rest of the originals drifted away. But it had lost several assets. First, it was clear there weren't enough players to keep more than a single team going. Second, enquiries from overseas had more or less dried up – the novelty of Icelandic cricket appeared to have worn off. Third, there wasn't anywhere in Reykjavík to play. Having staged matches outside the city at Tungubakkavellir in 2000 and 2001, and at Víðistaðatún in 2002, the team had been allowed to use the national sports stadium at Laugardalur in 2003 – but that honour would surely not be bestowed on them again, now that the publicity stunts had all been staged.

All that exists from 2004 is a solitary newspaper image, apparently snapped by a passing photographer, of a bit of cricket in a park. Sammy is batting; vice-consul Minshull is keeping wicket. There are no Icelanders in the photograph. This was a foretaste of the future. Until now, 60 players had appeared for Iceland or its three local teams: 50 were native Icelanders, and 10 were immigrants. Of the next 60 to make their debuts, only five would be Icelanders.

It was only by the unlikeliest of coincidences that the Iceland cricket team stirred again, through a chance meeting at a European aluminium conference in Germany, early in 2005. Over a boozy gala dinner in Essen, two Englishmen got talking about cricket. One was John Clarke, the editor of the *Aluminium Times*, and the other was Barry Woodrow, a supplier of smelting equipment, who had become (after Dharmendra and Sammy) the third expat to play cricket in Iceland. As the beers were downed, a wager was raised: £100 to whoever could assemble the better team. Clarke in England, or Woodrow in Iceland.

The teams were indeed assembled, and Clarke's group – named after Ovingdean, his home village in Sussex – signed up for a chilly weekend in Reykjavík. Woodrow, with the help of Ragnar and Benedikt, got an Icelandic team together; vice-consul Minshull dragged the artificial pitch to the Klambratún park. Criss-crossed by tarmac paths, and strewn with dogs and their doings, Klambratún was an unlikely cricket venue: the dog-walkers looked on in bemusement as white-clad Englishmen totted whiskey from hip flasks and stood about an uneven pitch, clapping their cold-stung hands.

Two games were played. In the first, Iceland impressively but embarrassingly managed to lose their last seven wickets without scoring a single run and, despite dismissing four Ovingdean batters with the score on one, rapidly lost the advantage, and ultimately the match. Ragnar and Benedikt scored ducks, and vice-consul Minshull, charged with the task of getting the opposition out, tried to bowl faster and faster, all the while being baited and goaded by the visitors' top-scorer, Richard Teasdale, "who never shut up for one minute". Next day, Ovingdean very sportingly reversed their batting order, with Teasdale once again driving vice-consul Minshull nuts during a rollicking innings of 51. Nevertheless, thanks to their guests' generosity of spirit, Iceland were able to draw the series; a neat conclusion, albeit one which left the matter of the £100 wager unresolved. This would gnaw at Woodrow and Clarke for the next few years.

"I came to the conclusion that aluminium guys are like the Americans," muses Ragnar. "They just hate to see a draw and will go to any lengths to finish what they started." That length would turn out to be about 4,000 kilometres.

The following year, cricket awoke again, but in an even more unlikely location. The Icelandic government had decided to construct an enormous hydroelectric power plant at Kárahnjúkar in the remote central highlands, hundreds of kilometres from the nearest town. The project was overseen by the engineering company Impreglio which, in 2006, brought in a hundred workers from India and Pakistan, all of whom were allowed to bring their families with them, if they wanted to (most didn't). An isolated and self-sufficient community sprang up, with its own school, shop and hospital.

Unsurprisingly, given their provenance, the workers started to play cricket (in summer, at least; in winter the temperature at Kárahnjúkar could easily fall to –25°C). They even formed two teams: Kar-11 (the dam builders) and Kar-14 (the tunnel diggers). Their organiser, Ómar Valdimarsson, challenged Kylfan to a match. Ragnar accepted the challenge – but Impreglio wouldn't give its workers the time off.

Cricket was still deemed newsworthy by its very presence in Iceland. Having reported on the pick-up games being played at Kárahnjúkar, the press were also delighted to report that students at the University of Agriculture in Hvanneyri had played cricket at their end-of-summer fair.

Ragnar knows nothing about this.

"To be honest, I would not be surprised if they actually played croquet," he says. "We often found that the media confused the two. No matter how much we tried to explain they were different games, they didn't seem able to grasp that there were two sports with similar names. Even today, I think most people in Iceland think they are the same."

Another stag party came in 2007: a group of Englishmen who worked for DHL in Sweden. There was an attempt to pass this off as the first international cricket match between Iceland and Sweden but, this time, the press didn't bite the bait. Ragnar was not altogether surprised.

"Well, we were still the comedy news item," he says. "We never made it to the back page. The newspapers were deeply suspicious of us ever since 'Iceland beats England at cricket', so it was hardly surprising they didn't take us seriously. The only surprising thing was that the rest of the world did."

The DHL men got hammered the night before the game, and consequently hammered on the pitch the next day as well.

Ragnar was certainly content with the way things were going. His friends may have drifted away from cricket, but he still had an affection for the game, and an annual match against a touring team satisfied his hunger admirably. Benedikt was similarly enthusiastic, and keen to honour his great-grandfather's reputation as the godfather of Icelandic sport by remaining the secretary of the ICA – even if a double-figure score continued to elude him (he made 7 against DHL).

Ragnar had moved on from his insurance job to take a post at Eimskip, the national shipping company. One morning, not long after the DHL game, he arrived at his desk to discover a young Indian man occupying the desk opposite. Tata Consultancy – the largest Indian company in the world – had arrived in Iceland.

If you are a cricket fan (or a fan of steel manufacturing), you will have heard of Tata. At the same time that the Icelandic banks were splurging their money – or more accurately, other people's money – all over the world, Tata was also expanding. It had bought Corus Steel, in the biggest corporate takeover by an Indian company, and had expanded into Iceland. Suddenly, Iceland had Indians.

THE FIRST DOZEN MATCHES

Saturday 22 July 2000 at Stykkishólmur
Stykkishólmur won by 11 runs
Stykkishólmur 60. Kylfan 49.

Saturday 19 August 2000 at Stykkishólmur†
Kylfan beat Stykkishólmur

Saturday 9 September 2000 at Tungubakkavellir†
Iceland won by 13 runs
Iceland 107. Utopians 94.

Saturday 28 July 2001 at Tungubakkavellir†
Kylfan won by 58 runs
Kylfan 111. Tryggingamiðstöðin 53.

Saturday 17 August 2002 at Víðistaðatún
Tryggingamiðstöðin won by 79 runs
Tryggingamiðstöðin 172. Kylfan 93.

Friday 18 July 2003 at Laugardalur
Effigies beat Kylfan
The match was played at midnight.

Saturday 19 July 2003 at Laugardalur
Effigies won by 54 runs
Effigies 183. Iceland 129.

Effigies then played on Langjökull glacier.

Sunday 20 July 2003 at Stykkishólmur
Effigies won by five wickets
Stykkishólmur 109. Effigies 110 for 5.

Sunday 17 August 2003 at Stykkishólmur†
Kylfan won by 88 runs
Kylfan 138. Stykkishólmur 50.

Saturday 13 August 2005 at Klambratún
Ovingdean won by five wickets
Iceland 59. Ovingdean 61 for 5.

Sunday 14 August 2005 at Klambratún
Iceland won by three wickets
Ovingdean 94. Iceland 100 for 7.

Saturday 16 June 2007 at Klambratún
Iceland won by 61 runs
Iceland 158. DHL (Sweden) 124.

† Icelandic Cricket Cup

V

EXPATS

A FRIEND OF ICELAND IN THE HISTORY BOOKS
Friend of Iceland and cricket player Sachin Tendulkar set a
world record today in a game between India and South Africa.
Tendulkar is the first man to score 200 points in one day (in
cricket, it is considered good for a player to reach 100 points in
one day). Tendulkar is considered the most admired son of India.
He spent a week in Iceland during his summer vacation last year,
playing golf in Mosfellsbær. Of course, our photographer was on
the spot and snapped on a photo of the occasion.

Morgunblaðið, 24 February 2010

Let us make no bones about it. Cricket lives in India. It may have
been born in Iceland, but it has long since moved to India (the
English may make spurious claims about being the 'home of cricket'
if they wish).

It took some time, though, for Indians to visit the birthplace
of their game. By 2007, only two had played cricket in Iceland:
Dharmendra, and a friend of Sammy's named Bharat Singh. But in
the autumn of that year, Benedikt was walking through Klambratún
when he came upon a surprising sight: a group of Indians playing
cricket, using the footpaths as a pitch. No Dharmendra, no Bharat;
Benedikt didn't recognise anyone. On enquiring, he was told that
they'd just arrived in Iceland, and they worked for Tata. He asked
how many they were.

"About eighty," came the reply.

Front and centre among the new arrivals was a man named Sanjoy
Karturi. He was (as everyone is) surprised to discover that cricket
already existed in Iceland; even more so to learn that it was run by
native Icelanders. Over the winter, Karturi was put in touch with
Ragnar, and they agreed to stage an exhibition match, when the
following summer began in earnest.

The Icelandic summer can rarely be said to have begun, mind you, and never in earnest. The snow may recede some time between February and May, but it can return at any moment, and temperatures often fall below zero, even in high season. Indian cricketers are slow acclimatisers in more temperate conditions overseas, and the sub-Arctic climate is some way short of temperate.

Early June in 2008 was far from clement. Rain and wind abounded. The Tata players insisted on playing a Twenty20 game, the first time this format had been played in Iceland, but found the elements – not to mention the rolled-out pitch on lumpy park turf – hard to handle. At least they bowled first, which meant they started well; Kishore Padmanabhan took the first five-wicket haul in Iceland, as the locals crawled to 74 for 9. But home teams understand their conditions, and they know what a winning total is. Tata reached 26 without loss, then were skittled for 54. Dharmendra claimed 4 for 15 and a young Nepali, Anil Thapa, took 2 for 5.

Even so, Tata's players were undaunted. Their view was that a game's a game; the result a mere footnote. Their delight upon discovering they had been posted to a cricket-playing country, and their enthusiasm to play regardless of conditions, proved infectious among the locals. Ragnar and Benedikt readily agreed to Karturi's proposal for a summer tournament. Kylfan's kit was dusted off, as was the Icelandic Cricket Cup, for a quadrangular T20 competition between two Kylfan teams and two Tata teams. From next to nothing, Icelandic cricket was about to have its most active season yet. It would scarcely have been imaginable twelve months earlier.

The tournament started badly for Kylfan, with both their sides beaten by Tata's B team. Then both clubs' senior teams faced, and defeated, their inferiors. Kylfan B lost their last game, claiming the wooden spoon, and setting up a decider between the two A teams. It was a thriller. The whole competition had been played without the artificial pitch, on a rudimentary mown strip of grass at Klambratún, and bouncers not only felled but hospitalised two players. Kylfan needed 35 runs from the final 20 balls, which came down to one from the last; a madly dashed single saw them home. Three teams thus tied the tournament with two wins each; there is no record of how the tie was broken, or indeed whether it was broken at all, but Tata would have clinched it on net run-rate.

The tournament is noteworthy as the first proper cricket competition in Iceland. It began ten days after the first Indian Premier League final and, as the Tata players saw it, was well on the way to becoming the IPL's biggest rival.

News then arrived from England that the Ovingdean team wished to return to Iceland to settle their bet – now three years old. Woodrow and Clarke's wager was tied at one match apiece, and the latter hoped his team, reinforced by a couple of ringers, could force a result in his favour. £100 is a lot of money, even to aluminium tycoons.

This time, Clarke's men were completely outgunned by the thriving Icelanders. They prepared for the big event with a triangular round-robin. It was an inauspicious warm-up. They lost to Kylfan, then were stuffed by Tata, who recovered from 35 for 6 to rack up 203 (a new national record) and win by 153 runs. Taking things increasingly seriously with every game – how very Indian of them – Tata put together a highly professional display to brush Kylfan aside in the final match, despite a testing and timely three-wicket haul from the grand old man himself, Ragnar.

Ovingdean now had to face the Iceland national team in an attempt to win Clarke his bet. Sportingly, the locals tried to assemble an eleven that was as close as possible to the side that had faced the tourists three years earlier; none of the Tata men were included. It didn't help much; Ovingdean were thrashed, and Woodrow pocketed his winnings. The final ball of the match was bowled by Ragnar, hit high by Ovingdean's number eleven, and caught by Benedikt. It was the final moment of their cricketing careers.

It shouldn't have been, though. In early August, the British Embassy was contacted by the officers of *HMS Exeter*, on a NATO patrol in the Atlantic. Instead of the customary 24-hour bender, taking in every strip club and clip joint in town, the seamen were keen to play cricket on Icelandic soil, and thus reprise the Royal Navy's event of 65 years previously (though hopefully not their defeat). It fell to vice-consul Minshull to organise the game. Once again, he dragged the pitch and scoreboard to Klambratún, for an anniversary fixture.

Just as the match was about to begin, it rained. It threw it down. Seamen and landlubbers alike ran for shelter, leaving the pitch and scoreboard where they were. Given the Icelandic climate, it is surprising that the first 26 cricket matches had taken place without any interruption for weather, but now, at last, the deluge came. It rained incessantly for a month. Nobody returned to Klambratún. The pitch and scoreboard were left where they lay and were never seen again.

They weren't the only things that disappeared in Iceland in the autumn of 2008. Everybody knows what happened next. The financial crash – locally known as the *kreppa* ('pinch') – was a traumatic time for all Icelanders. The króna collapsed, inflation doubled and unemployment tripled. Thousands of immigrant workers left. Among them were the Indians of Tata – every single one. Among them was vice-consul Minshull, who accepted a new diplomatic posting in Iran. Among them were Dharmendra and Sammy, Iceland's two original expat cricketers.

As the nation engaged in navel-gazing and soul-searching, there was little thought of cricket. Ragnar and Benedikt felt it was all over. They gave up their posts as chairman and secretary. No replacements were appointed. No meeting was held. Communications between players dried up. Within a few weeks of Iceland's most active season, its cricket scene was as dormant as two dozen of its volcanoes. The stewardship of Icelandic cricket – in name, at least – fell to perhaps the only man in Iceland not at the mercy of the banking crisis.

Lee Nelson was born in Perth, Australia. As a child, he was a talented cricketer, playing for Morley. Damien Martyn, the Australian international, was occasionally a team-mate. As an adult, he dreamed of a life outside the rat race. Blessed with natural athleticism, he began performing as a clown; proving so adept that he was soon in great demand. He even found himself booked to appear, on stilts, at an international game at Perth's largest cricket stadium. During an interval, a group of local children were brought onto the field to play, while Lee amused the crowd of 25,000 by clowning around on his stilts. When the ball – which was unusually large and rolled with a chiming sound – was hit towards him, he tried chasing it. The spectators' laughter turned to gasps of concern as the children chased it too, tangling with Lee's stilts and tumbling aside. It was only at that point that Lee realised the children were blind.

His act garnered so much repute that he was soon being booked to appear at festivals and events all over the world. Over a decade, he visited more than 100 countries, all at the expense of the corporate machine. Eventually it dawned on him that he had failed in his singular mission: he had, after all, joined the rat race.

It was a pivotal moment. He cancelled all his bookings and returned home to Perth in a quandary. While he was ruminating in front of the television, he saw – for the first time – the Eurovision Song Contest. This is a key event in the Australian cultural year, which makes it surprising that Lee had reached 30 years of age without having even *heard* of it. And he was entranced – not by the contest itself, but by the Icelandic contestant, Silvía Nótt, whose performance was a piece of high camp in a circus performer's outfit. Lee took this as a sign and packed his bags.

His journey from Perth to Reykjavík was far from easy. Only when his flight landed in London did he realise he needed to switch airports, and for that he needed a transit visa, which he didn't have. This is not the kind of thing British border guards let pass; these were people whose eyes flashed fire if you ticked one box incorrectly, and they put Lee through the mill. Rather than deport him to Australia, at the British taxpayer's expense, they decided to let him continue to Iceland – but blacklisted his passport. He would be Iceland's problem.

Lee arrived in a state of uncertainty. Surely the Icelandic immigration desk would not take kindly to the arrival of a man on the international 'banned' list. A frowning official picked over his passport.

"You are blacklisted."

"I know," replied Lee. "They did it in the UK."

"Oh, they did, did they?" Iceland's relations with the UK had not, historically, been very friendly. Iceland did not like the British dictating right and wrong.

"Why did you come here?" asked the guard.

Lee felt that honesty was the best policy.

"Well, I saw Silvía Nótt on Eurovision and thought this was a place I have to visit."

The guard paused.

"Welcome to Iceland," he said. "Have fun."

And Lee did. Iceland's banking rush was in full swing. Lifestyles were unfettered. Money was falling from the skies. The nightlife had a soundtrack: energy, stupidity in the streets. He got laid that first night, and never looked back.

After a year of such cultural acclimatisation, Lee placed an advert in a local newspaper advertising free headstand lessons. A dozen people showed up. This was the seed from which Sirkus Íslands – Iceland's first and only circus – began. By the summer of 2008, it was up and running. A big top, and a full tour schedule around Iceland, were yet to come, but there were regular practices and performances in Klambratún. It was on one such occasion that Lee saw the Indians of Tata playing. The joy of his cricketing youth was rekindled, and he joined in. He became a key player in that Indian summer, even being hospitalised after breaking his face in the Cup final.

Then came the *kreppa*. The expats repatriated themselves, the Icelanders hung up their milkmen's outfits – but in the circus, the show went on. Lee had by now met, and married, an Icelandic woman, and was thus a fixture on the cricket scene, which is more than could be said for anyone else. He effectively became chairman by default.

In the fallow years that followed, though there was no actual cricket in Iceland, there was certainly talk of it. In June 2009, *Morgunblaðið* reported that Sachin Tendulkar, the Indian superstar player, was in Iceland with his family. The 'Little Master' was quoted as saying: "I've travelled all over the world, but I wanted to think outside the box, do something different from what I'm used to, and travel to a country where cricket is a little-known sport. Two of my Indian friends had spoken very positively about Iceland and said it's a great place."

For Tendulkar, it was good news that Icelandic cricket was moribund. If he'd come a year earlier, he'd have been mobbed by Tata employees. As it was, he managed to keep his arrival under wraps; he wanted to play golf, not cricket. The local travel agent asked a golf-playing friend, an Englishman, if he'd be able to show Tendulkar around, and sort him out some golf lessons. By coincidence, that Englishman was Peter Salmon, the man who'd organised Iceland's first post-war cricket match, back in 1979.

Thirty years later, Salmon was no longer a cricket player, but had remained a follower of the game. Of course he knew who Tendulkar was – but he was sworn to secrecy. Not that it was necessary; Iceland was the first place Tendulkar had visited where he could safely use his real name at hotels, without risk of attention.

Salmon took Tendulkar to the best golf course he could think of, and organised lessons with the club pro. They began at the driving range. Tendulkar teed up and brought out a three-iron. The pro was about to intervene, but Salmon stopped him: this guy is an international cricketer, so he can probably hit this. The pro was sceptical. Tendulkar hit the ball 250 metres, flat and far.

A young boy was practising on the putting green, and Tendulkar noticed him missing a five-foot putt. He strolled over and bet the boy he could make the putt – then missed. Now the Indian showed his competitive side. He replaced the ball, tried again, and missed again. And again. Salmon, the pro and the boy watched and waited as Tendulkar, lost in his own little battle, kept attempting the putt. Only when he had sunk it five times in a row did he snap out of his trance and give the boy his putter back.

As they drove back to the city, Salmon found himself star-struck. He had the world's most famous cricketer to himself and could ask him anything. So many questions came to mind. Should he keep it simple? Career highlight, perhaps. No, too banal, too predictable. Should he be personal? Something about Tendulkar's family? No, too nosy, too impertinent. Overwhelmed by possibilities, he asked the driest question imaginable: what would Tendulkar like to do for dinner?

Perhaps surprisingly – perhaps not – Tendulkar said he would like to go for a curry. Posterity has not recorded what the manager of the Austur Indíafélagið restaurant said when he learned Sachin Tendulkar was coming for dinner, but it is known that he cancelled the evening's other bookings and ended up on his knees before the 'Little Master'.

Tendulkar was thus inducted by the Icelanders into the hall of fame comprising famous people who visited Iceland and liked it. The latter point is a must. The actor Emma Watson filmed in Iceland in 2012 and made unkind remarks about the local cuisine; she has been unwelcome ever since. Tendulkar joined the ranks of Bill Clinton (who had a hot dog named after him) and Justin Bieber (who had a car park named after him) in becoming a 'friend of Iceland'.

When, in February 2010, he became the first batter to score 200 in a one-day international, *Morgunblaðið* reported it with glee. The purpose of the article was not, of course, to report his cricketing achievement, but to remind the Icelandic people that Sachin Tendulkar had (a) visited Iceland, (b) liked it, and (c) had his photograph taken by the newspaper's photographer. And there, dear reader, you have the Icelandic mentality in a nutshell.

The paper even occasionally reported on the 2010 IPL – but only focusing on Tendulkar's performances, to the exclusion of all other information, and only for the purpose of reminding their readers that he had been to Iceland. It meant, at least, that many Icelanders knew the IPL existed, even if they didn't care. This came in handy when *Morgunblaðið* splashed its next scoop.

LALIT MODI MAY SEEK ASYLUM IN ICELAND

It is rumoured in the Indian media that Lalit Modi, the former Indian Premier League manager accused of corruption, will seek asylum in Iceland. Modi's wife is a good friend of the Icelandic First Lady, Dorrit Moussaieff. According to his lawyer, Modi is in mortal danger in India.

Morgunblaðið, 15 October 2010

Iceland has a history of this sort of thing. When the chess prodigy Bobby Fischer faced deportation to the United States in 2005, Iceland granted him citizenship, apparently for the sole reason that he had played the famous 1972 World Chess Championship there. Iceland's foreign secretary said there was a "certain feeling of solidarity with an exceptional champion who is having a hard time" and that Fischer had "helped put Iceland on the map". Edward Snowden, the CIA leaker and whistleblower, tried a similar gambit while on the run but, having milked the publicity for all it was worth, the Icelandic government eventually decided not to admit him. He hadn't been to Iceland, you see. The Modi story proves it doesn't really matter if the Icelanders have heard of you or not; if you're famous somewhere in the world, and you so much as *mention* Iceland, you're newsworthy. Unfortunately, the heat surrounding Modi's imminent arrival was swiftly doused.

LALIT MODI DOES NOT WANT TO COME TO ICELAND

Lalit Modi, the former Indian Premier League manager, will not apply for political asylum in this country. Modi's lawyers say the rumours have been spread by an angry client, and Modi wrote on Twitter that he is not interested in going to Iceland.

Morgunblaðið, 20 October 2010

You can almost *taste* the disappointment.

There was a solitary stirring from the slumbers during Icelandic cricket's latest hibernation. It came in the form of a team of eccentric Dutchmen known as the Fellowship of Fairly Odd Places. They had formed a few years earlier with a view to playing an annual match in one of cricket's unlikelier outposts. Their first match was at Baarle-Nassau, on a field straddling the border between Belgium and the Netherlands. Their next fixture was against a team of priests from the Vatican; then came a game on a North Sea sandbank at low tide. Iceland seemed a natural fit for the Fellowship, and they arrived on a gloriously sunny summer weekend in 2011, bedecked in red and white striped blazers which made them the talk of the town as they strode down Reykjavík's main street. Lee's increasingly popular circus now toured Iceland all summer, so his position as chairman was taken by an Englishman: a bioinformatics programmer (no, me neither) called Keith Hayward.

A barbecue was laid on at Klambratún as Robert Kottman seared the Iceland batting order, claiming 5 for 16 and performing the first hat-trick in Iceland. The locals were bowled out for 117, but they knew better how to bat on their dodgy lawn than the Dutchmen did, and defended their runs adroitly. Thapa sealed victory with the last two wickets. The gracious visitors presented every Iceland player with a signed, framed bat. Three years had passed since a cricket match had been played in Iceland – and three more would pass before the next.

Hayward occasionally managed to get a handful of hardcore enthusiasts to turn up for a knockabout in Klambratún, but the ICA records show that 2012 was a particularly lean year. Team communications were typically limited to the question "how many of you are around for cricket?" and a positive response only from Thapa.

THE NEXT DOZEN MATCHES

All 20-over matches (except in 2011), and all played at Klambratún

Wednesday 4 June 2008
Iceland won by 20 runs
Iceland 74 for 9. Tata 54.

ICELANDIC CRICKET CUP
11 June to 3 July 2008

Tata B won by 61 runs
Tata B 157 for 9. Kylfan A 96.

Tata B won by five wickets
Kylfan B 72. Tata B 73 for 5.

Kylfan won by five wickets
Kylfan B 143 for 6. Kylfan A 144 for 5.

Tata won by five wickets
Tata B 107 for 6. Tata A 108 for 5.

Tata won by eight wickets
Kylfan B 60. Tata A 61 for 2.

Kylfan won by three wickets
Tata A 125 for 9. Kylfan A 126 for 7.

THE TRIANGULAR TOURNAMENT
Saturday 5 July 2008

Kylfan won by five wickets
Ovingdean 118 for 9. Kylfan 119 for 5.

Tata won by 153 runs
Tata 203 for 9. Ovingdean 50.

Tata won by five wickets
Kylfan 81 for 6. Tata 82 for 5.

Sunday 6 July 2008
Iceland won by 65 runs
Iceland 166 for 7. Ovingdean 101.

Saturday 9 July 2011
Iceland won by 26 runs
Iceland 117. Fellowship of Fairly Odd Places 91.

Things weren't much better the following season, though in fairness to Iceland, it had another sport on its mind: 2013 was a breakthrough year for Icelandic football, as the men's national team came within a match of qualifying for the world cup. Having held Croatia to a goalless draw at Laugardalur, they went down 2–0 in the away leg and broke the hopeful hearts of a nation. Their time, of course, would come. Thapa and Hayward swapped roles; that is, Thapa – as chairman – would ask who was around, and Hayward would furnish him with the only positive response. There might be another, if Lee wasn't on the road with the big top.

The wake-up call came early in 2014, in the form of an unlikely request from a team of Australians – and not just any Australians. Victorians. Or at least, the state's over-60s team. They were going to a team-mate's wedding in Ireland and had decided to arrange fixtures in Dublin and Kilkenny. It seemed logical to make a quick trip over the border to play in Belfast and, once there, a mere hop over the Irish Sea brought the prospect of cricket in Scotland. Their itinerary became longer and longer, eventually encompassing five matches in Ireland, four in Scotland and more than three weeks on the road. What difference would a 1,600-mile round trip to Iceland make?

Thapa assessed his resources. They didn't look good. Hayward was increasingly busy with work and Lee was touring with the circus. The usual email enquiries yielded the usual silence. It was at this moment that Facebook launched in Iceland. This proved one of the two catalysts for the recovery of cricket in Iceland. The other was the first person to get in touch using it.

Abhi Chauhan was born in Delhi and had played cricket throughout his childhood. A cricket obsessive, he was always desperate to play, but never joined a club. After leaving school, he travelled to Switzerland to study hospitality and tourism management. There, he met his future wife, half-Russian, half-Icelandic, and when she returned to Iceland, he came with her, taking a job as a bartender at the 1919 Hotel in central Reykjavík. It was there, during a quiet morning shift, that he joined Facebook and discovered, to his surprise, that there was cricket in Iceland – and a match in the offing. He could not have known it then, but he was the right person in the right place at the right time.

Facebook brought further good news. Jakob Robertson, born in Sydney to an Icelandic expat and her Australian husband, had grown up with cricket. He'd played for Narrabeen – at the time, the worst team in the Sydney suburbs. After over a decade in Australia, Jakob's mother had become homesick: pining, if you will, for the fjords. It was decided that the family would up sticks and move to Iceland. Jakob learned of the plan when he came home from school to find a 'for sale' sign outside their house.

Jakob was thrown in at the deep end: a new country, a new school, and a new (and impenetrable) language to learn, all at the age of twelve. But his classmates were fans of *Neighbours*, and were delighted by his arrival, and took to him eagerly. It was the summer of 2001, and almost as soon as they had arrived, Jakob's mother read the article in *Morgunblaðið* announcing that Sky would be covering a local cricket match. Jakob's father – also a cricket fan – took him along to Tungubakkavellir to watch. They were interviewed by the Sky crew and featured in the final broadcast.

After graduating in forestry from the University of Agriculture, Jakob – who, if not quite a hippy, had become something of a man o' the land – went travelling, as men o' the land usually do. On his return, he joined Facebook, and stumbled upon Icelandic cricket.

Two oven-ready cricketers were exactly what Thapa needed. Others got online and came out of the woodwork: another Indian, a Sri Lankan, more Englishmen and Australians, even a willing Icelander. They were confronted with not only a highly talented opposition comprising state-team veterans, but the obligation to play on the unprepared grass at Klambratún. Most cricketers have played pick-up games in parks or on backyard lawns, but attempting a proper match on such a surface is fraught with danger. The turf at Klambratún was so uneven, it may as well have been corrugated iron. Four of the Victorians were hit by the ball and retired hurt. Injured batters were walking to and from the nearby hospital as frequently as fit ones were walking to and from the pitch. The entire touring squad – sixteen players – were allowed to bat, and none scored more than 15. But these veterans, though pensionable and in triage, provided a real and ultimately insurmountable challenge to the Icelanders. What they lacked in youthful fitness, they more than made up for with experience and cricketing nous. They made the locals sweat for their runs. Jakob made a modest 10, perhaps worth 50 in the circumstances; Abhi was hit in the face and suffered a fractured eye socket. At least he had company in the hospital waiting room. Chasing Victoria's 113, Iceland needed four from the final ball. Their sole Icelandic player swished and missed, so had to try and run four. He was run out going for the first.

One thing was clear: if cricket was to continue, a better pitch must be found. Nobody really knew where to start. There were four types of grassy field in Iceland, and all had their faults: parks (full of potholes and paths), pasture (full of sheep), football pitches (full of football) and common land (full of jagged lava rocks and, if local folklore is to be believed, invisible elves).

At the end of 2014, Thapa moved back to Nepal, so Abhi took the reins. He'd moved into an apartment in Kópavogur, just to the south of the capital, which he shared with his wife and his cricket obsession. He badgered the town council for a few months, to no avail. It probably didn't help that he wasn't Icelandic and couldn't speak the language. As winter set in, he hit upon the idea of splitting the lead role in Icelandic cricket: he would be the organiser, but Jakob would lead on the field. Having an Icelandic captain would be a great boon for public relations. Jakob was only half Icelandic, of course, but was fluent, and his Australian surname was only one 's' short of being legit.

It worked. With Jakob as the poster-boy, and Abhi doing the legwork, the ICA was permitted the use of Sporthúsið ('The Sport House'), a small hall with wooden walls and a green carpeted floor, normally used for handball. It seems hardly believable that, for a decade and a half, nobody had thought to practise cricket indoors, but at last there was a way to train during the winter.

Under Abhi and Jakob's stewardship, Icelandic cricket grew not only in size, but in strength. Over the next two years, social media enabled visiting teams to arrange tours, and newly-arrived expats to join the scene. The core of today's Iceland national team began to take shape.

Four teams came to Iceland in 2015: Columbia from New York, Carmel from Wales, Galah from Australia and Dollar from Scotland. Of these, the Americans were by far the strongest. Their squad included an engineering student called Ashwin Venkatakrishnan, who had played youth cricket for Bangalore, in India. He was almost certainly the best batter to set foot on an Icelandic cricket field since Captain Grace – but Iceland had acquired their own secret weapon.

Nolan Williams was born in the Caribbean, in 1970. Like so many West Indians of that time, he grew up watching the region's great fast bowlers – the likes of Michael Holding, Malcolm Marshall and Curtly Ambrose – dominate and terrorise all comers. Like so many, he wanted to emulate them – and he was built for it, too. Tall, sinewy and strong, he loved bowling fast, and could work up quite a pace for Questelles Rangers, his local club. Unfortunately, he was from St Vincent, a cricketing backwater as far as the West Indies were concerned. The country had reared a handful of decent international players (Cameron Cuffy, who played 56 times for the West Indies, was a contemporary), but Nolan wasn't picked up by the coaches' radar. The next best thing was to make it as a professional; Wilf Slack and Neil Williams hadn't cut it at international level, but both Vincentians had forged long and successful careers in English domestic cricket.

Nolan's chance arose after he had moved to Antigua to work (and play cricket) for the police. English county cricketers came visiting on a pre-season tour, and he attracted the scouts' attention. Like Neil Williams, Nolan threw in his lot with Essex. His trial at Chelmsford came in 2000, the year after his namesake retired. His played his first game under the captaincy of Peter Such, who had played eleven times for England, and it went well: he took four wickets in a friendly match against Hertfordshire and earned himself a call-up for the Second Eleven Championship match later that week.

Luck was not with him. After bowling just a few overs, he suffered a shoulder injury that kept him out for a month (and which plagued him for the rest of his cricketing life). On his return, he had lost a little pace. Though he played alongside the likes of Michael Carberry, Tim Murtagh and Ed Joyce – who hit him all over the park at Harrow – he didn't make a big impact and wasn't signed. Perhaps his shoulder wasn't up to it. Perhaps, at 30, he was too old. Either way, he resigned himself to an alternative career as a banker. It can't have been a hardship. He rose through the ranks, was talent-spotted by an Icelandic bank (and an Icelandic woman) in the wake of the *kreppa* and moved to Reykjavík. He was the first of Abhi's recruits from a relentless social media trawl.

Even at 46, he was still the fastest bowler yet seen in Iceland. His tussles with Venkatakrishnan during the Columbia tour were the stuff of legend. Sporthúsið was far too small for fully-fledged matches, so Abhi booked the massive Kórinn sports hall. A huge atrium, covering a full-sized football pitch, it had been used to host concerts by the likes of Andrea Bocelli and Justin Bieber. Its artificial turf was covered in rubber crumbs – ideal bounce for football, but lethal for facing a fast bowler. Still, the boundaries were short, if a batter took on the challenge. Venkatakrishnan won the face-off convincingly, scoring 67, 85 and 78 as Iceland were put to the sword, tying the first match but losing the next two. This was high-octane cricket – but when dealing with genuinely good players, something a little more subtle, even strategic, was required.

David Cook, a Devonian, grew up bowling left-arm seam for the village of Harberton. An introspective, cerebral type – he studied sustainable development at Exeter University – he found himself at odds with striving, swaggering league players. When he relocated to London, he switched to finger-spin and enjoyed a much gentler cricketing existence with Battersea Bohemians. But he soon heard the siren call of Iceland: its whales (and geothermal power stations) were too much to resist for an academic of environmentalist bent. It was an unexpected bonus to stumble upon Abhi's recruitment drive.

His analytical eye and tactical variations were exactly what was needed. Abhi quickly realised that, to harness the full power of David's flight, games needed to be played on a larger field. For the visit of Carmel, the matches were relocated to Kórinn's outdoor pitches. These were still rubbery and bouncy, but with long boundaries: an ideal combination for spin bowling. It was possible to score runs, but only with patience. After Iceland narrowly won a frenetic T20 game, the teams decided to play a longer fixture, and it was in this match that a Pakistani mechanic by the name of Mohammad Younas scored 114, the first century for Iceland, who racked up 276, a new record. This gave David plenty of time to settle into a long, match-winning spell.

When Galah visited, the three-match series (Hayward's final games) was level at one apiece, and it was agreed that the third should be a long-format game. The Iceland team felt, for the first time, that they had a winning strategy. Patient top-order batting – David himself scored 118 in the decider, having been asked to open because he was the only player willing to leave a good ball – would give way to lower-order hitting. Lee, whose athletic gifts made him an obvious choice as wicketkeeper, would then try to hit quick runs. So would Abhi, whose favoured position was number seven because, in his own words, "you can just go in, not listen to anyone, and do what the hell you like". Nolan would open the bowling, as fast as he could, to try and blast out the batters, and David would toss the ball up and try and catch them in two minds. To Jakob fell the task of captaincy, putting all these bits and pieces together.

Though Galah won that final match, they were given quite a scare, and they weren't altogether happy about it. They had come for a few beers and a laugh, and wondered if they'd been hustled. The truth was, the Icelanders were as surprised as their Australian visitors.

Dollar, the team from Scotland, turned out to be very good. They had already gained an upper hand by turning up wearing kilts, which many of the locals had never seen before. They capitalised on this mental advantage by wearing them to practise. It was September – the beginning of the Icelandic winter – and though the Scots were happy to play outdoors, the Icelanders weren't (none having been born further north than their guests). So back inside they went, neutralising their advantages and costing them the game. Lee was out first ball, Jakob top-scored with just 25, and once Dollar had seen off Nolan, they laid into David. Iceland may have had five players of genuine quality, but that was still six short of a good team.

Those six players were unearthed over the winter. Now indoor practices were taking place, Abhi reasoned he could arrange indoor matches. He resurrected Kylfan Krikket Klúbbur Reykjavíkur and gave it a snappier name: Reykjavík Vikings. They needed a team to play, so he formed a new one, named after his home town: Kópavogur Puffins. This was something of a misnomer, since Kópavogur means 'Seal Pup Cove' and has no puffins, but one of Abhi's many idiosyncrasies was a cast-iron determination never to learn Icelandic, so Puffins it was. With about half a dozen players on each side, the teams played two indoor series, one in late 2015, and the other in early 2016. Kópavogur won both series 3–2, but the main legacy of those contests was the completion of the modern, full-strength Iceland international team.

It may not have happened so soon, if at all, were it not for the Myllan bakery in Reykjavík. In the wake of the *kreppa*, and the exodus of European workers that followed, grassroots Icelandic companies were desperate for cheap labour. The bakery was managed by a Sri Lankan woman, and she called on her nephews for help. Lakmal and Dushan Bandara had recently finished school back home in Kandy and, out of a sense of family duty, took up the night shift. They were still only teenagers, and found the cold, dark environment lonely and forbidding; when they discovered Icelandic cricket on social media, they jumped at the chance to get involved in something familiar. Both were hard-hitting all-rounders: Lakmal, the elder, was right-handed, and Dushan left-handed. They had grown up playing for the Black Knights, the pre-eminent team in Kandy's tennis ball cricket league, a prominent competition with cash prizes. Never before had they played with a real cricket ball.

Neither had their countryman Chamley Fernando. Also from Kandy, he represented the Sisu sports club as a swing bowler, but had suffered a shoulder injury and decided to reinvent himself as batter and wicketkeeper. He had been training as a carer for disabled children when he learned of an opening for an au pair with an Icelandic family.

Keenan Botha grew up in the Mitchells Plain suburb of Cape Town. Both his parents were mixed-race, and he led a happy and free childhood, playing cricket alongside kids of all races at Avondale. His dream was to become a footballer but his father, a priest, insisted cricket would make him more of a gentleman. A talented left-handed batter and spinner, he was playing two-day cricket by 16; soon he was on the radar of Western Province. Just as he felt a professional contract might be a real possibility, his life took an abrupt turn: his father announced they were moving to Iceland in search of a better life. Keenan struggled with the news, and wondered if he would ever be able to find an identity in such an unfamiliar place. The sporting dream seemed over; occasional football games were all there was – or so he thought. One evening, hanging back in defence, he was called over by his team's hyperactive Indian goalkeeper. "You're from South Africa, right? Do you play cricket?" It was Abhi.

The next to turn up was Derick Deonarain, a 22-year-old hotel worker who had just arrived from Guyana, where he played club cricket for Albion, on the Berbice coast. He longed to be a fast bowler, but his diminutive stature prevented him putting pace on the ball. He had instead become a technically exemplary batsman, off-spinner and brilliant fielder, and had played regional cricket at youth level. Of all Abhi's early recruits, Derick was the closest to a complete cricketer.

Leslie Dcunha, from Bangalore, was the final piece of Abhi's jigsaw. Tall and rangy, he had represented the state of Karnataka at basketball; unlike the others, he had come to cricket late, beginning when almost twenty. His only club cricket had been a summer camp with Bangalore Gymkhana. But he had a good eye and the coolest of temperaments, and when he came to Iceland – via a Swiss hotel management school – he went along to a practice session in the spring of 2016 and found himself a new hobby.

With these core players in place, the strength of the Iceland team improved rapidly. Masstor, a works side from England, visited in the summer of 2016, and were battered like dead fish meat among the rubber crumbs of Kórinn. Abhi and Jakob decided their team should try and find their true level – and that would necessitate leaving Iceland. International cricket, though, seemed a step too far, so the decision was taken to enter a club tournament: the Pepsi Cup, held annually by the Czech Cricket Union.

Sirkus Íslands – or rather, Lee – put up the money for a coloured playing kit. But with no other sponsors, each man had to pay to play, so it wasn't quite a full team that travelled to Prague in September. David, Leslie and Nolan couldn't make it, and the appeal of Czech hospitality – and beer in particular – had a limiting effect on the capabilities of the eight who could. They started badly, losing to Geneva, Doha, Vienna and Evergreen (a Pakistani expats' association in Sweden). But then they beat Winterthur, and Geneva in the fifth-place playoff. And they had, through trial and error, worked out broad roles.

Derick and Leslie were suited to opening the batting: a left-hand, right-hand combination who could build a secure foundation. Keenan, Dushan, Lee and Chamley formed the big-hitting middle order, then Jakob and Abhi would work it around at seven and eight. Nolan's pace and Dushan's left-arm swing made them ideal to share the new ball; the change bowlers would be Lakmal, for line and length, and Abhi, for a repertoire of variations. The spin attack comprised left-arm darts from Keenan, and droppy drift from David. Lee kept wicket, with Chamley as his understudy; Abhi, Derick and Jakob would prowl and pounce inside the fielding circle. It was no longer a team, but a unit.

By the time the 2017 indoor series came along, these regulars were now playing T20 games under the roof at Kórinn. All 11 featured in the decider in April; Reykjavík chased 148 to take the series 3–2. As the summer drew close, the decision was made to appoint a specialist captain for the first time: Derick was given a two-year tenure, Jakob became chairman, and Abhi was charged with the task of organising Iceland's first tour to England.

VI

DEBUT

Oh God. They have a cricket team as well.

Michael Vaughan, former England cricket captain, after Iceland
beat England at the European Football Championship, 2016

Everyone has a bad year. Mine was 2016. Having enjoyed a happy
decade and a half as a teacher, I've been on the wrong end of a
scandal of tabloid-press proportions, and though I come out of it
untainted and financially compensated, I've lost my job and my
mental health.

I spend the winter feeling distinctly sorry for myself and try to
envisage some semblance of a future. After the front line of teaching,
it's hard to readjust and I feel ill-equipped to start a whole new
career. The education system loves to recruit trainee teachers from
professional backgrounds, regarding them as boasting the full gamut
of skills: people, management, communication. The reverse is far
from true. Teachers, once released into the wild, find it hard to transfer
to other workplaces. They need more structure than they get. They
crave variety. They talk down to people, forgetting that not everyone
is a fourteen-year-old who has forgotten their textbook again.

I can't imagine being in an office. I don't know how I would fit in.
I taught geography, coached cricket, ran a debating society, helped
out with school plays, staged quizzes, edited the school magazine,
interviewed prospective new teachers and pupils, mediated
disciplinary hearings, compiled timetables and organised an annual
trip to Iceland. A jack of all trades, perhaps, and master of none.
As I contemplate my next step, there are two things I feel I can't
do without: being involved with cricket and visiting Iceland. I'm
completely, obsessively, infatuated with both.

I was twelve years old when cricket first bit me. It was 28 June
1991, a Sunday morning, and I'd wandered into the kitchen to
find my mother riveted by something on television (my mother

watched television from a day bed in the kitchen, for reasons I never understood). I was surprised, I recall, because it wasn't a soap opera. My mother watched everything – *Eastenders*, *Neighbours*, *Eldorado* – but there was usually some respite at the weekend. On this occasion, my mother was transfixed by cricket. I'd never seen her watching sport before.

"It's very exciting," she said. "England are playing the West Indies, and we're definitely going to lose."

"How is that exciting?" I asked, not unreasonably.

"Because the West Indies can't finish us off," she explained. "We're about seventy runs ahead, and if two more England batsmen are out then the West Indies will have to go in and get an easy score to win."

"Right."

"Which they will."

"Right."

"But they can't get these two out. They're called Pringle and Lewis. And the West Indies just keep bowling and bowling but they aren't getting them out. It's wizard fun!"

My mother spoke like an Enid Blyton novel.

"So we could win?" I pressed.

"Oh, no, we won't win. But it's fun watching the bowlers not being able to get these two out."

So I watched. And, perhaps contrary to my childish expectations, it *was* fun. Derek Pringle batted five hours for 45, and Chris Lewis hit 65 at number ten. They extended the lead to 152, after which Phil DeFreitas had the West Indies 24 for 3. England still lost, but it was enough. I was hooked.

In the following game, at The Oval, I watched Viv Richards' farewell, Tufnell's incredible spell of 6 for 25, the West Indies losing seven wickets for 18 runs, 'Syd' Lawrence's marathon five-fer and Botham's 'leg over' hit wicket dismissal and match-winning runs.

It took me another six years to learn how to play cricket, but throughout secondary school I umpired, scored, and enthusiastically practised when any of the 'real' players would let me (which was seldom). I devised my own cricket statistics database, I played cricket computer games until the controller buttons were worn to stubs, and I read every cricket book I could lay my hands on. As soon as I went to university, I started my own cricket team and captained it for the next twenty years, eventually becoming really quite a decent bowler.

One of my team-mates was another cricket badger, somewhat older than me, a hugely charismatic raconteur and devoted Marxist by the name of Daniel Norcross. He was a comfortably well-off management consultant – how he squared this with being a Trot was a mystery nobody ever solved – who cured his nine-to-five office-block ennui by starting *Test Match Sofa*, an irreverent cricket commentary service. When he launched it, in the summer of 2009, I was one of the founding participants. Since I was a teacher, I had vast amounts of time to commentate on the Sofa during the school holidays. The broadcasts were enormously popular and bred a whole new generation of cricket media figures, including Vithushan Ehantharajah, Jarrod Kimber and Nigel Henderson. Norcross himself was eventually snapped up by the BBC's *Test Match Special*.

Having been provided, courtesy of my employers, with a potentially infinite school holiday, I wondered if I could get into professional commentary somehow. More in hope than expectation, I went through some old Sofa tapes and sent a few clips of myself to the BBC. Their reply was encouraging. "It shows plenty of promise," they said. "But we need an idea of what you'd sound like doing a longer spell of commentary at a venue." So I took a digital voice recorder to The Oval and sat in an empty stand on the first day of a County Championship match, and recorded myself describing the most uneventful passage of play imaginable. I think eight runs were scored for no wickets. The BBC told me they "very much enjoyed the recording", and would keep me in mind. Two months later, on my 38th birthday, I found myself wearing a BBC polo shirt in the commentary box at Taunton, picking up a live microphone for the first time as Sidebottom bowled to Trescothick. Cricket was now my career.

I met my other great love at university. She was distant, frigid and uncomfortably damp. She was also pretty big – about 100,000 square kilometres – and had a population of 350,000. I first visited Iceland on a glaciology expedition, spending five days in the pouring rain measuring lichens on the sediments of a valley glacier. Amazingly, this didn't put me off. There was (and still is) something breath-taking about the sheer scale of Iceland's vast and barren wilderness. Seeing mile upon mile of sand, ice and lava rock, the vista unbroken by trees, has a profound and stupefying effect. It is not quite beautiful, but the landscape inspires a deep sense of awe. I took friends to see Iceland, and later, as a teacher, I took my pupils, and was always rewarded by the dumbfounding effect of their seeing Iceland for the first time.

Since there was little likelihood of cricket commentary paying any bills, I decided to sustain my infatuation with Iceland by starting a travel company, bringing people over the Atlantic to see the island for the first time. Thus I embarked upon two careers simultaneously, as cricket broadcaster and tour operator, often remarking to friends what unlikely companions these two vocations were. On air at Taunton, the local commentator Anthony Gibson asked me what my "day job" was. "I organise tours to Iceland," I said. For a brief moment he seemed startled. "Cricket and Iceland? That's an unusual combination." He was right.

⁂

"Can you do something for me?"

Abhi is a man of many catchphrases, but none sums him up better than this. He's quite a hustler: as a child in India, he never played for a club, but instead organised his own tournaments, which he considered "the best way to make money in India during the summer". How could anyone else have kept Icelandic cricket alive through hard times, let alone grown it? Over three years, he has doubled the number of clubs (to two), players and touring teams. What he needs now is money. When we first meet, in a café in downtown Reykjavík, he talks of little else. He's looking for sponsors for the tour of England, which is just a few weeks away. I ask how many backers he has so far.

"Lee is going to give us some money from the circus. And Leslie manages a clothing company. So he's going to sort us out with some new jerseys."

That sounds like a good start to me. He means playing jerseys, right?

"No, like polo shirts, to wear on the plane. The playing jerseys are being supplied by an English company called Viking Cricket."

That sounds good too. What's the deal?

"If we buy our playing jerseys from them, they will give us £1 for every bat they sell."

I reckon Viking Cricket has done very well out of Abhi.

"You have a travel company, right?" he asks.

"Well, it's a start-up. I've only had a couple of clients so far. Friends. Couples. Nothing big."

"Yes, but it's a company, right? You can sponsor us. We need caps. Can you get us caps? Cricket caps? Like proper, modern ones?"

My company does not manufacture cricket caps but, all the same, Abhi has unknowingly exploited a weakness. I'm a cricket cap badger. I love them. I collect them. I bite the bait.

"Ooh, so like, a nice, brushed cotton six-panel cap, with an embroidered badge." I must sound like a proper knob.

"Whatever you say. Look, I'm from Delhi. When people talk about the design, I talk about price. You give us the caps, and you can put your company logo on them."

I think about suggesting Abhi buys the caps from me, in exchange for £1 for every holiday I sell, but managed to quell the impulse.

"Okay, Abhi. And you'll give me the Icelandic Cricket Association logo, to put on the front?"

"Ah, you will have to make something. We don't have a logo yet."

This is the first – and the least – of many surprising things I will hear from Abhi over the coming years. The ICA has existed for 18 seasons and has no logo. Even the two domestic teams have one: Reykjavík have an image of an angry, bearded Norseman, and Kópavogur have a rudimentary drawing of a puffin sitting on a wicket. But the national team have never had caps, and if I'm to sponsor them, I have to come up with a badge.

"Is there anything else I can help with?"

"You tell me." That's Abhi.

Fumbling for other ways to be useful, I mention that I have just started to work as a BBC commentator. There might be an opportunity, at some point, for Icelandic cricket to feature on air.

I've made a suggestion that does not involve money, and Abhi is unimpressed. He has a tour to run and doesn't think media coverage will be much help. Besides, there's been little outside enthusiasm for Icelandic cricket. I later count 25 appearances in the media up to

2017, of which 20 have been in the local press – mostly in Icelandic – and three on blogs. Only two overseas outlets have shown any interest: *The Times*, when Tim Dellor visited in 2001, and the BBC, when their commentator Henry Blofeld came with the Effigies in 2003. That was a long time ago.

Abhi brightens for a moment.

"Do you think the BBC will sponsor us?"

I suggest this is unlikely.

We agree to reconvene in England: Abhi with the rest of the team, and me with the caps.

The tour is hosted by Elstow Cricket Club, just outside Bedford. It seems a curious landing spot for a national team, but I'm informed that someone from the club sent a speculative email to Abhi, and he ran with it. All the regulars are in the touring party, except Chamley, who has had problems obtaining a visa. A sponsor's teenage son, Elliott, is roped in to make up an eleven.

In the first match, somewhat incongruously, Iceland's opponents are Bedfordshire Young Farmers. They are better than they sound: in 2022, Sir Alastair Cook, England's leading Test run-scorer, will play for them. Derick, in his first match as Iceland captain, plays a starring role, taking three wickets as the Farmers make 122, then scoring a crucial 30 to take Iceland home in the final over. Elliott hits the winning runs.

The next day, Iceland begin their three-match series with Elstow. There will be 20, 50 and 40 over games during the weekend, beginning with an evening game on the Friday. Floodlights are rigged up for the T20 encounter, and Elstow struggle to 95 for 8 as the sun sets. Dushan and Nolan, steaming in with the new ball, keep the scoring down, and Abhi's all sorts pick up wickets. Derick decides to go for quick runs, and packs the top order with his hitters – but the plan backfires. Lee, Keenan and Derick himself are out to wild shots, and the home bowlers scythe through the order. When Nolan is dismissed, Iceland are a woeful 20 for 7. But the Bandara brothers turn the situation around. They add 70, but both are run out in the penultimate over, leaving the last pair to find three from the 20th. Neither has yet faced a ball, but both are competent: Leslie, usually the opening batsman, has been dropped down to number ten; Abhi can give the ball a whack and runs like the wind.

There follows an almighty choke. Leslie fails to score off the first and second balls but races a single from the third. Abhi swishes and misses at the fourth and fifth but manages to steal a bye. The scores are level, Leslie is back on strike, and all they need to do is run. Abhi, at the other end, reveals himself to be a hustler in more ways than one. He tears off his helmet, gloves and pads, declaring that he can run faster without protective gear. He is within his rights, under the laws of cricket, but the Elstow fielders aren't having it. It is a situation which often arises in modern cricket: the upstartish Indian exploits a technicality to gain an advantage, and the stentorian Englishman accuses him of being unsporting. Today, the English prevail, and Abhi sulkily puts his gear back on. It doesn't matter in the end: they throw to Leslie's end, run him out, and the game is tied.

Saturday brings another good contest: an all-day game, beginning before lunch, with 50 overs per side. It's quite a big ask after the exertions of the previous evening, and Nolan's shoulder gives up the ghost halfway through his fourth over. Matthew Stevens, the Elstow opener, scores a century, but Dushan and Derick take three wickets each, and Elstow are all out for 227. In reply, Iceland have another nightmarish start; of the top four, only Elliott bats with any comfort. But, from 44 for 4, the Bandaras stage another rescue, putting on 50. When Lakmal goes, Jakob helps Dushan add another 61. The runs flow steadily, but time ebbs faster, and the score is 208 for 9 when the overs run out. Elstow have gone 1–0 up in the series, and all the Icelanders can hope to do is equalise on the Sunday.

The day dawns with good news and bad news. Nolan is fit enough to play, though he won't be able to bowl. But David has been struck on the arm in the practice nets – and a precautionary trip to the hospital in Bedford has revealed a break. Even with Elliott, Iceland are down to ten men.

Abhi is the messenger.

"We need you to play." He throws me David's kit. "What do you bowl?"

As it happens, I am the closest thing to a like-for-like replacement. Like David, I bowl spin. Like David, I toss the ball up, slow and high. Like David, I rely on the batsman possessing a dodgy temperament: impetuous and impatient, ideally.

My first proper coaching was in 2000, when I was at university. Once a week, a friend and I would drive to Taunton, the nearest county cricket ground, for lessons with a top-drawer Somerset coach. Except we couldn't afford a top-drawer coach, so we were put under the tutelage of Andy Hurry, a former Army physical training instructor taking his first coaching certificate. He had us in one net (my friend batted, while I bowled; we never swapped) and a younger lad named Peter Trego alongside. Hurry intended to turn me into a swing bowler. Having taught me accuracy and variation, his parting words to me were: "Now you know how to bowl. Next year we'll get you a proper run-up."

I never went back. Thanks to Hurry's tutelage I could drift the ball at very slow pace – no more than 40 or 45 miles per hour – and batters would lose their cool. My club captain told me there was only one thing I needed to know about batters: "They have no powers of self-control whatsoever." To this day, I regard these as the wisest words a slow bowler could ever hear. My variations were subtle: a dipping off-cutter and a quicker outswinger. Over time, when I realised I was never going back to Hurry, never destined to bowl any faster, these became a backspinner (a late-Victorian era favourite, long forgotten, delivered by cutting the fingers under the ball, so that it drops in flight and jumps at the batter) and a more conventional arm-ball, which occasionally and accidentally came out like a doosra.

Before my lessons at Taunton, I had tried my best for three seasons, taking 11 wickets for my club at an average somewhere in the mid-thirties. After Hurry had finished with me, up until my debut for Iceland, I took 434 wickets at 13 apiece. I was even in the local paper once, after recording figures of 9 for 1 against Kingston one Sunday afternoon.

But Elstow are a big league club, and a different prospect entirely. I'm not accustomed to this standard. For a start, spin bowlers at this level fire it in, flat and fizzing. That's how Derick and Keenan bowl, too. I toss my deliveries so high they can down drones. David assures me I will be fine. He knows the self-control principle, too, and reminds me that rushes of blood are not exclusive to the social player.

It's a 40-over game, and Derick decides Iceland are better off chasing, since that's what they've got used to. It's hard to say exactly what target would instil confidence, but they have not yet raised 100 without the loss of at least five wickets. Dushan swiftly removes both openers, then Derick and Abhi reduce Elstow to 28 for 4 before the recovery begins. Their captain, Phil, leads the fightback alongside a nuggety number six. It doesn't take Derick long to realise I cannot throw, so he brings me in close to the bat. I misfield and have to run back for the ball. Lee, keeping wicket, barks at me.

"Sloppy, mate!"

It's my first experience of being admonished on the field by a hard-nosed Australian. None of the "bad luck, Kit" or "on it next time, Kit" here. How pathetically English. I've been sloppy and I've been told. Suddenly Lee is my father, and I'm a disappointment. I go red, and quiet.

The fifth-wicket partnership has reached 42 when Derick – somewhat reluctantly, I sense – tosses me the ball and beseeches me to "keep it tight".

I can recall every detail of my first over for Iceland, not least because some thoughtful soul on the boundary recorded a video of it. It's not the bowling itself that stands out – six stock balls, all on a length – so much as the soundtrack. It is obvious from what follows that I have a style with which neither the Icelanders nor the Elstow men are familiar. A style that not even David's twirlers have prepared them for.

Ball one. Phil plays far too early outside off stump and misses. Lee collects. "Wow, that was slow."

Ball two. Phil defends from the crease. "Okaaay," says Lee, still somewhat dubious.

Ball three. Phil advances down the pitch, thinks better of it, and defends again. Someone laughs loudly.

Ball four. Phil hangs back and blocks once more. Lee turns to Lakmal, at slip. "What the hell *is* this?" Lakmal shrugs.

Ball five. A little shorter. Phil shapes to play to leg, misses and is hit on the pad. An appeal from afar – probably Abhi. Derick asks Lakmal why the ball isn't being hit into the trees – and demonstrates how he would do it. Lakmal shrugs again.

Ball six. Phil can bear it no longer. He takes a stride towards me and drives with all his might. The ball pops back to me, making a satisfying smack as I catch it. Abhi cheers and races to me, arms outstretched and pumping. My team mates look at each other. Phil looks at the ground.

In my second over I bowl the number six. I haven't yet conceded a run. "Who's this bowler?" asks one of the spectators, evidently worried. Elstow are all out for 112, and I finish with 2 for 17, the best figures of the game. Though Iceland endure another bad start, reaching 40 for 4, Derick stays calm and sees the chase through, with Lakmal hitting three late sixes. Iceland have won their first game in England, and I'm delighted with my debut performance. Elstow's captain is as lavish with praise as only a vanquished batsman can be: "Watching you bowling, you just think, why doesn't this guy go for six every ball? And then you're facing it, and suddenly it's much harder." Lee and Derick overhear and raise their eyebrows. I'm not sure they're convinced.

The tour's final fixture is a little different, and it's not immediately clear how Abhi found it. The hosts are Eton Ramblers, the venue Eton College. The Icelanders have grasped it's a school, but none – except David, the sole Englishman – is prepared for the grandeur. Eton College is England's most famous private boarding school. It was originally founded – like many of England's private schools – to support the education of poor children. The annual fees now exceed £40,000, and alumni include Princes William and Harry, plus 20 British prime ministers.

Eton College owns most of the town and a sizeable portion of the surrounding countryside, much of which acts as the pupils' sports fields. They have arcane, unusual names (the sports fields, not the pupils – no, scratch that, the pupils have them too). Football is played at Mesopotamia, hockey at Old Master's, rugby at Dutchman's, and something called 'field game' at Agar's Plough. The cricket ground, rather disappointingly, is called Upper Club, but by the time we reach it, most of the Icelanders are stunned. So this is their school? But they *live* here? How many pupils are there? *Twelve hundred?* Do they each get their own football pitch?

"Guys, we are in real England now," says Abhi. "Don't break anything."

"Don't even *touch* anything," laughs Leslie.

"Fuck that. If it's not nailed down, take it," says Lee.

We are greeted heartily by an Old Buffer, whom we learn has been Abhi's correspondent in arranging the fixture. His appearance

Professor Terry Gunnell, the leading expert on Viking pastimes at the University of Iceland.

[Kit Harris]

Síminn á afgreiðslunni er 83033 Morgunbladid Sími á ritstjórn og skrifst 1010

LAUGARDAGUR 20. OKTÓBER 1979

Mikið atvinnuleysi er á Eyrarbakka

Eyrarbakka, 19. október.
EKKERT hráefni hefur borist til Hraðfrystistöðvarinnar á Eyrarbakka undanfarið og var síðasti vinnsludagur 9. október. Síðan hafa um 40 manns verið á atvinnuleysisskrá. Togarinn Bjarni Herjólfsson hefur verið bilaður og er nú í slipp. Ekki er búist við, að hann komist á veiðar fyrr en e.t.v. um miðja næstu viku. Í kvöld er von á 17 tonnum af síld til stöðvarinnar, en það magn

hrekkur skammt ef ekki kemur meira til. Annars hefur atvinna verið með besta móti hér það sem af er árinu.
Nánast ógerningur er að fá hráefni til vinnslu um þessar mundir og má því búast við lélegu atvinnuástandi hjá fjölda fólks hér á meðan togarinn leggur ekki afla á land. Einn línubátur leggur upp afla hjá Einarshöfn og sá fiskur fer til harðfiskvinnslu og í salt.
—Óskar

Söltun tvöfalt meiri en í fyrra

BÚIÐ er að salta í um 60 þúsund tunnur af Suðurlandssíld samkvæmt upplýsingum, sem Morgunblaðið fékk hjá sildarútvegsnefnd í gær. Er það tvöfalt meiri söltun en á sama tíma í fyrra.
Í vertíðarbyrjun tókust samningar um fyrirframsölu á um 135

árum, og eykur það því líkurnar á því að landað verði meira af hringnótasíld en í fyrra.
Samkvæmt sölusamningum atvinnuvegsnefndar hefur sala verið tryggð á öllum þeim stærðarflokkum, sem leyfilegt er að veiða.

Krikket á Melavelli

Þeir eru margir kappleikirnir sem fram hafa farið á gamla Melavellinum og í gær var þar í fyrsta skipti leikið krikket, þjóðaríþrótt Englendinga. Eins og sjá má á myndinni eru leikmenn í fullum skrúða við leikinn sem fór fram af sérstöku tilefni. Sjá íþróttasíðu.

How the national press reported Iceland's first modern cricket match, at Melavöllur in October 1979.

[*Morgunblaðið*]

The first Kylfan team, at Stykkishólmur in July 2000.
Back: Eyjólfur Sigurðsson (12th man), Ragnar Kristinsson (captain),
Sammy Gill, Siggi Jónsson, Dharmendra Bohra, Stebbi Ásmundsson,
Steinar Haraldsson (umpire), Stefán Pálsson, Kári Ólafsson.
Front: Ólafur Unnarsson, Benedikt Waage, Valur Gunnlaugsson, Jóhannes Númason.
[Ragnar Kristinsson]

Iceland beats England at cricket: Jóhannes Númason bats against the Utopians
at Tungubakkavellir in September 2000. Marcus Rule is keeping wicket.
[Morgunblaðið/Jim Smart]

Twelve-year-old Jakob Robertson, who went on to captain Iceland, is interviewed by Sky Sports alongside his father, during the Icelandic Cricket Cup at Tungubakkavellir in July 2001.

[Sky Sports]

The Icelandic Cricket Cup at Víðistaðatún in August 2022.
Left to right: Ragnar Kristinsson (wicket keeper), Jóhannes Númason (striker),
Ágúst Hauksson (non-striker), Stebbi Ásmundsson (umpiring), Barry Woodrow (bowling).

[Jón Svavarsson]

Cricket on a glacier: Henry Blofeld, Andrew Imlay (seated), John Williamson, Robert Mitchell and Jonathan Stocker of the Effigies team, July 2003.
[*Morgunblaðið*/Jim Smart]

A member of the Iceland Express publicity team bats on the Langjökull ice cap.
[*Morgunblaðið*/Jim Smart]

Indian and Pakistani workers take a break during the Kárahnjúkar dam project, in June 2005.
[Ómar Valdimarsson]

Iceland play Ovingdean at Klambratún in July 2008.
Dharmendra Bohra bowls, and Lee Nelson keeps wicket.
[Anil Thapa]

The artificial pitch has been lost, but cricket goes on at Klambratún. Mohammad Younas bowls against the Fellowship of Fairly Odd Places, in July 2011. Keith Hayward is keeping wicket.
[Anil Thapa]

Bala Kamallakaran, who will become chairman of the Icelandic Cricket Association in 2021, bats against the Victorians at Klambratún in July 2014.
[Anil Thapa]

The indoor pitch at Kórinn claims another victim: Iceland v Columbia, May 2015.
[Abhi Chauhan]

The Iceland team celebrates victory over Winterthur on
their first tour, to Prague in September 2016.
[Icelandic Cricket Association]

The publicity blitz begins: Sammy Gill, Sathiya Rupan, Venkatesh Kumar
and Jakob Robertson model the new kit at Kleifarvatn in June 2018.
[David Powell]

Sammy Gill, David Cook, Jakob Robertson, Lakmal Bandara, the owner and Prabhath
Weerasooriya during a publicity shoot for a kitchen showroom in England, July 2018.
[Kit Harris]

From the old to the new: Ragnar Kristinsson, the first chairman of the
Icelandic Cricket Association, faces his successor, Lee Nelson.

[Guðmann Þór Bjargmundsson]

Víðistaðatún – the Meadow of the Willow – in Hafnarfjörður, before its conversion.
[Kit Harris]

The world's northernmost cricket ground (64.07N) opens on 26 May 2019.
[Kit Harris]

The Watch by Timo Solin.
[Kit Harris]

The world's northernmost scoreboard.
[Kit Harris]

Prime Minister Katrín Jakobsdóttir prepares to face the first ball.
[Kit Harris]

Abhi Chauhan
[Sathiya Rupan]

Chamley Fernando
[Sathiya Rupan]

David Cook
[Sathiya Rupan]

Derick Deonarain
[Martyn Haworth]

Dushan Bandara
[Kit Harris]

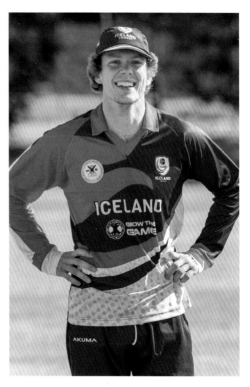

Jakob Robertson
[Sathiya Rupan]

Keenan Botha
[Sathiya Rupan]

Kit Harris
[Sathiya Rupan]

Lakmal Bandara

[Sathiya Rupan]

Lee Nelson

[Sathiya Rupan]

Leslie Dcunha

[Kit Harris]

Nolan Williams

[Martyn Haworth]

Prabhath Weerasooriya
[Kit Harris]

Sadun Lankathilaka
[Sathiya Rupan]

Sammy Gill
[Kit Harris]

Darren Talbot, the coach.
[Kit Harris]

The Iceland squad at Valletta, Malta, in 2019.
Back: Darren Talbot (coach), Derick Deonarain, Keenan Botha, Lakmal Bandara,
Sadun Lankathilaka, Leslie Dcunha, Prabhath Weerasooriya, Kieren Lock (physio).
Front: Lee Nelson, Sammy Gill, Kit Harris, Nolan Williams (captain),
Lakmal Bandara, Jakob Robertson, Abhi Chauhan.
David Cook and Chamley Fernando did not travel.
[Kit Harris]

Seven of the originals at Kenilworth Road, Luton, in 2019.
Kári Ólafsson, Valur Gunnlaugsson, Stebbi Ásmundsson, Ragnar Kristinsson,
Stefán Pálsson, Benedikt Waage, Siggi Jónsson.
[Kit Harris]

is typical of his type: ruddy face, Panama hat, striped blazer and deck shoes. I fancy I detect a whiff of gin. We're directed to our dressing room. The pavilion is so immaculate, Nolan wonders whether we should observe the Icelandic custom of removing our shoes before entering.

"I feel like even my socks will spoil the floor," says Abhi.

Derick loses the toss and, for the fifth time in a row, Iceland are fielding first. Nolan's shoulder is playing up again, so he has enlisted a junior player from Elstow to take his place. While the rest of us get changed, Nolan and David make small talk with Old Buffer – or rather, listen to Old Buffer talk. Every private school's old boys' club has an array of Old Buffers, who have two essential topics of conversation. One involves reverentially dropping the names of a dozen famous people with whom they have recently lunched, but of whom you have never heard. The other involves describing in detail the cricketing pedigree of every player enlisted by Old Buffer, who is keen to put it on record that they're all much, much better than you.

Abhi, Lee and I are the first out of the pavilion. Old Buffer is talking Nolan and David through his eleven.

"We've got Abbott. He's a blue. He'll open with James. MCC, you know. Boyd, too. And Freddie Fox. He's the captain. And a blue. O'Brien, county cricketer. Bruce, county cricketer."

"Wait, you have first-class cricketers in your team?" I ask. "Professionals? How many?"

Old Buffer has a think. "Nine, I think."

He shuffles away. I turn to the others.

"Nine?" I groan. "We're going to get *thrashed*."

"Good luck!" grins David. Having a broken arm doesn't seem so bad after all.

"What's a blue?" asks Abhi.

"Who gives a shit?" replies Lee. "Let's get out there and fuck them up."

It is the English custom that the home team choose which format to play, and Eton decide on a timed game: 60 overs in total. The side batting first can declare their innings closed if they like; they can only win if they bowl out the side batting second, so they must give themselves enough time to do so. The Iceland team have only ever known limited-overs or, in the early days, play-to-a-finish matches.

A timed game is an entirely alien concept – and there is much furrowing of brows. So the match could end in a draw? Who wants a *draw*? No Icelandic team has ever played out a draw.

We bowl well early on, and take a couple of wickets, but that is as far as our buoyancy goes. Eton's scoring soon becomes rapid, and Derick decides to turn to spin, so he and Keenan take the ball. But the runs come faster and faster. Abbott scores a quick fifty, as does W. R. C. Gordon-Lennox. The run-rate rises above seven an over, but Derick perseveres. As the score rockets towards 200, I ask if I might have a bowl – I'd done quite well yesterday. Derick just looks at me, blankly. Other players suggest plans. Lakmal wants to bowl. We could even give Jacob a go. But our captain is in the zone. Quite what zone, it's hard to say. Every suggestion is met with an impassive glance and wordless rejection. He bowls and bowls, and Eton hit and hit. It's an impressive display of single-minded masochism.

After less than two hours, Eton declare at 201 for 5. They have only faced 27 overs, but are observing another English custom. In a friendly match – that is, a match not being played for league points, or in a tournament – hammering your opponents is simply not done. Unless they're well known to you (in which case rivalry is permitted to trump friendship), manners dictate that you should go no further than 200. If the other side can get there, then three cheers for them. Eton have evidently decided we *won't* get there, in which case it is wise to give themselves 33 overs to bowl us out.

During the tea interval, our team divides into two groups: one looking up the professionals we are playing against (this group comprises David and me) and the other discovering that private schools traditionally serve port during tea (everyone else). Both groups make noteworthy discoveries. David and I establish that, contrary to Old Buffer's bragging, there are *no* professionals in his eleven, and the rest of the team become convinced of the medicinal benefits of fortified wine. Nolan, who has lived in England and, as a banker, has experience of this sort of thing, rises and proposes a handsome toast to our hosts, since our tour manager and captain are indisposed (Abhi has become too friendly with the bottle to be capable, and Derick is still not speaking to anyone). Lee, by no means a foe of the grape, is a particularly zealous convert to Eton ways.

It is unclear whether Lee sees the thunderbolt that has him caught at the wicket from the third ball of the innings. There are bleary eyes on the boundary, too, but a rapid sobering occurs when Keenan is leg before wicket from the sixth. There is general agreement that the bowler, Rory MacDonagh, is the fastest most of us have ever played against. It is immediately clear that, facing this formidable weapon, we cannot possibly win. To his immense credit, Freddie Fox, the Eton captain, reaches the same conclusion, and quickly relieves us, so as to conjure a contest (good English social teams are highly adept at manipulating friendly games to engineer a close result, even if not in their favour). More humane bowling is introduced, enabling Derick and Dushan to nurse the score up to 90 for 4. Fox gives himself a bowl. His spin is innocuous, but accurate, and he sends back three batsmen – and runs out Jakob – in the blinking of an eye.

We are 90 for 8, with six overs remaining. Dushan, still going well, marshals the strike so the young lad from Elstow has little to do. He gets carried away, hitting four sixes, and prompting the reintroduction of MacDonagh for the final over. The Elstow boy is on strike and sees it through; while disappointed not to have been called on to bowl, I am delighted not to have been required to bat.

There is further port after the game – strictly ceremonial, to mark the end of the tour – but the Icelanders are eventually poured out of the pavilion, affectionate goodbyes are bade to Old Buffer, and promises are made to return in a decade or two. I make my way to my car but hear a yell behind me. Abhi is chasing me down.

"Can you do something for me?"

We've been here before. More caps?

"You have a travel company, right?"

VII

TOURISTS

The things I think about most during the day are death, cricket and sex. Probably in that order.

Sebastian Faulks, on Icelandic television, 2017

Abhi is an ideas man. But whatever powers of motivation and persuasion he has – and he has them in abundance – he is not a logistics man. Things fall into place, or they don't, but the tune of chaos is always in the air. Twelve teams have toured Iceland, the last five at Abhi's invitation, but the effort involved is overwhelming. Every team wants advice about flights, local transport, hotel bookings and sightseeing, before a ball is even bowled.

"Mate, these guys always want help with everything," he says. "In 2015, I said yes to everyone who wanted to come. We had four teams, and it nearly killed me. So last year, I just invited one. But they still needed help with everything. My boss was going crazy, my wife was going crazy. Now Jakob is chairman, and we have four teams coming in 2017, and he isn't a travel agent any more than I am. So can you do something?"

It's pretty good timing. My company is only a few months old, and needs clients. Helping Jakob out with his touring teams will solve both our problems, and I'm only too happy to accept his suggestion that I become the ICA's official tour partner. I contact all four teams, offering my services. Two decline – they have everything in hand, thank you very much, and need no assistance – but two accept. I have my first tour groups.

Hackney Village are an occasional side, whose specialities seem to be playing cricket overseas, and drinking alcohol overseas. In the ten years of their existence, they have toured in Amsterdam, Ireland, Corfu, and Croatia. This is a team who take their socialising seriously. I fix up a three-match T20 series with the Iceland national team: fly in on Wednesday, play an evening game, go sightseeing

100

on Thursday, two games on Saturday, then swim in the Blue Lagoon and go home on Sunday.

I don't immediately cover myself in glory: by screwing up the coach booking from the airport, I make the Hackney Villagers an hour late for their first game. Their chairman, John, is less than impressed, and the unprepossessing appearance of Kórinn's outdoor football pitch does little to ameliorate his mood. I attempt to mollify him by promising it'll be a wonderful game. And it is – though not for *his* team. Dushan scores a national record 127 from 45 balls, hitting 16 sixes, and only stops when the umpire persuades him to show a little mercy and retire (I am the umpire). Dushan is a genial, generous, amiable man, but cannot fathom why anyone would willingly stop batting without being got out, and departs with an air of bemusement. It is the first 'retired out' in the history of Icelandic cricket. I feel a little guilty, but the look of relief on the Hackney players' faces reassures me I've done the right thing.

Derick smashes a quick 32, but no one else reaches 20. Not that it matters – there is surely no way Hackney are going to overhaul a total of 230. Nolan, whose shoulder is having one of its good days, generates terrifying bounce from the springy surface and grabs two quick wickets. Derick changes the bowling, introducing new ammunition – a Sri Lankan spinner with a mesmerising array of variations.

Iceland's Sri Lankan population have not so much a family tree as a forest. Chamley's cousin has married an old schoolfriend from Kandy, named Prabhath Weerasooriya, and they live among the hot springs at Hveragerði, about an hour from the capital. Prabhath runs a tour company, bringing his countrymen to Iceland, which means we find common ground straight away. And he has a forensic interest in mystery spin, which only strengthens our affinity. He has learnt his tricks playing for the Brothers sports club, in a tennis ball league. It's vastly easier to master the art of wrist and finger spin with a tennis ball, and Prabhath can conjure all manner of magic. The tourists collapse to 24 for 6, but Derick has learned a great deal at Eton, and realises his duty with cheer. He gives everyone two overs, and Hackney have a hit, reaching 106 for 7 by the end. Unshackled by the need to compete – they now know they will not – the tourists relax considerably. In this they are assisted by the first two dozen of 144 cans of beer they bought in the airport's duty free shop (there were cries of anguish when the first sips revealed the main ingredient to be blueberries, but these were swiftly drowned). They depart for the city centre, and I promise to meet them outside their hotel at nine o'clock next morning.

I am there, bright and early, with my minibus. We are to see the Golden Circle, the mandatory day trip for any first-time visitor to Iceland. It takes in the earthquake fault at Þingvellir, where the Norse had their parliament, the erupting springs at Geysir, and the mighty waterfall, Gullfoss. On the home leg, there is usually time for an outdoor swim in naturally hot water, either at Gamla Laugin, Iceland's oldest swimming pool, or in the stream at Reykjadalur. It all makes for a really memorable day.

Whether the Hackney Village team will remember any of it is questionable. At 10 a.m. the first few appear, not from the hotel, but from the city centre. There has evidently been no sleep. Breakfast is declared the priority, followed by the rounding-up of stragglers, at least one of whom apparently *did* go to bed, just not at the hotel. At length, nine more or less upright cricketers board the bus. Two more are loaded into the luggage compartment, alongside a hundred cans of blueberry beer.

I have resolved be mindful that I am not a geography teacher any more, and adult tourists do not need to have the full out-of-your-windows-you-will-see monologue every second of the journey. I will drive, and leave them in peace. That's the plan, anyway. But there is no one as curious as a drunken man. Before long—

"Kit, what's that tower?"

"That's the Hallgrímskirkja, Reyjkavík's most famous church. For many years it was the tallest building in Iceland. There's a viewpoint at the top. Would you like to stop?"

"Nah."

A few minutes pass.

"Kit, what's that mountain?"

"That's Esja, a basaltic plateau, which the locals like to climb on a clear day. It's about 900 metres high. Would you like to stop?"

"Nah."

A few minutes pass.

"Kit, what's that glass building?"

"That's Hlaðgerðakot. It belongs to the health association. It's a treatment centre for alcoholics. Would you like to stop?"

Laughter. The sound of cans opening.

The consumption of blueberry beer becomes the preoccupation of the day. It is, by all accounts, undrinkable, but this only seems to fuel the determination to drink it. John makes it clear that he expects every drop to be finished, otherwise there will be penalties, which may involve purchasing more of it. The two unconscious men in the luggage compartment are spared the ordeal. The beauty of Iceland whirls by in a haze of blueberries and burps.

A long soak in the hot waters of Gamla Laugin proves restorative, to the Hackney men and to my reputation as a tour operator, as I assume the role of drinks waiter and ferry cans from the minibus to the pool. Plans are made, without hope or sincerity, for the following day's cricket. Strategising gives way to singing, which diminishes to a burble of blueberries as we return to the hotel. Every can has been defeated, without even having to rouse the two who, despite coming with us, have missed the whole day.

Come Saturday afternoon, the call is for a sociable, low intensity match. Derick, with a new-found affection for stat-padding, agrees to a timed game instead of two T20s, the longevity of which is thrown into jeopardy when Hackney Village win the toss and elect to bat. Prabhath spins his spell again, no one makes more than 15, and the tourists are all out for 67. The Icelanders knock the runs off in mere minutes, with only two wickets down. John insists we play on, partly because the best part of the afternoon is left, and partly because he is mid-way through a nice little bowling spell and has just got Derick out. So on we play. John is then carted all over Kórinn by Dushan, who hits eight more sixes in his 73, and Iceland reach 251. Hackney go in again, 184 behind, and manage 107, with Derick sparing them any further torment at the hands of Prabhath. The tour is, all things considered, a success, even if the cricket has been one-sided. I have safely led my first group round Iceland, and brought them home in one piece.

Not all the tours go so well. The two teams I'm not helping have a somewhat chequered experience. Allez Les Bloggers are such easy meat in their first game – Derick pounds them for 111, and Dushan blasts 67 from 29 balls – that several of the Iceland players, including

Derick and Dushan, don't bother turning up for the second. Allez Les Bloggers beat Iceland's eight-man team easily. It's not all roses for the Antelopians, either. After Jakob impresses on the Icelanders the need to be good hosts and show up, the full-strength eleven turns out – the first time they have all appeared in the same team – and the Antelopians are stuffed. The second day's cricket is scotched when it emerges that Abhi has forgotten to book the pitch.

The last of the 2017 visitors are the Authors, one of the most storied English clubs. Founded in 1891, the original team included several household names, including Arthur Conan Doyle, A. A. Milne and P. G. Wodehouse. After a 100-year hibernation, the team was revived by literary agent Charlie Campbell and novelist Nicholas Hogg. They have already visited India and Sri Lanka, played two national teams (Japan and Vatican City) and – naturally – published their own book. Their fame has even reached the shores of Iceland: this year they have been invited to the Reykjavík Literary Festival. The chance to tick off another national team is too good to miss.

This could be the ICA's biggest break since Bruce Dickinson flew in. None of the current players were around then, so I tell Jakob and Abhi this is a golden opportunity to get decent media coverage, in Iceland and overseas. All the Authors will be willing to 'do press' for them. We agree a three-match T20 series, played under the roof at Kórinn, for the Halldór Laxness Trophy. The only Icelandic Nobel laureate, winning the Literature prize in 1955, Halldór seems a fitting point of convergence.

The Authors arrive with an impressive line-up. Campbell and Hogg are accompanied by the best-selling Sebastian Faulks, historian Tom Holland, sportswriter Jonathan Wilson, children's author Anthony McGowan, cricket publisher Matt Thacker, philosopher John Sutton, and musician Roger McCann. Peter Frankopan, another historian, hasn't been able to make it, so a good club cricketer from London has been called in as a ringer. Steve Cannane, travelling and playing with the Authors, is covering the tour for the Australian Broadcasting Corporation. McGowan will report for ESPN, and Faulks for *The Spectator*.

Driving rain and wintry gusts accompany us to Kórinn for the evening game. We're grateful for the roof, though it still sounds like we're under a waterfall. The Icelanders are almost at full strength

– the lone absentee is Nolan, nursing his shoulder. The Authors win the toss and decide to bowl, so as to get a feel for the bounce. Iceland start well, reaching 42 for 0 before Hogg and Sutton work out how a bowler thrives indoors – pitch it up and swing it. They tear through the order, and the score is 58 for 7 when they finally meet some resistance. Leslie and Jakob, the two Icelanders who prefer accumulation to all-out attack, are perfect for the situation. They play themselves in, working hard for ones and twos until they are comfortable, at which point Leslie allows himself some big hits. They bring the total to 103 for 9, which they know must be enough. Kórinn has become a fortress for the home team, the rubber crumbs a minefield. McGowan hits Dushan's first ball to Jakob, who nearly takes a blinding catch at cover. The second delivery is an inswinging yorker, and McGowan is palpably leg before wicket. But Nolan's not here, so perhaps there will be some respite at the other end.

Sadun Lankathilaka was born in Colombo: a quiet, studious boy who sang in the school choir and played for the Shining Star cricket academy. He emigrated to Iceland as a child – like Jakob and Keenan, thrown in at the deep end. Two metres tall, dark-skinned, and speaking no English, let alone Icelandic, he found it hard to fit in. He fell into fights, drink and drugs. He got into trouble with the police. While on probation in 2006, in a drunken brawl outside a bar, he put a man in hospital and was sentenced to a year in prison.

Now married, and a father, Sadun is manifestly a new man. He is, as I am soon to discover, a superb cook and – surprisingly, given his giant stature – a beautiful singer with a high, gentle tenor. Even so, I wouldn't want to cross him. He is a giant, a man-mountain.

This by no means represents 'respite at the other end'. He is as fast as Nolan, but instead of relying on bounce, he bowls full on leg stump from around the wicket. Delivering the ball from a height of around eight feet, he is quite a handful. The Authors did not expect this. Nor did they expect the fleet-footed fielding which yields three run-outs, or the belligerent send-off Abhi gives Hogg when he has him caught behind. Other than a heroic 18 from Cannane, no one makes double figures. It is all a lot more serious, and less sociable, than the visitors thought.

The match finishes a little before midnight, and the Authors haven't eaten yet. They've had a drink – that much is clear since the bottle of Jameson's whiskey Derick had begged me to bring from duty free is empty. Abhi, having promised to provide a buffet dinner, produces with a flourish a box of 100 Toffee Crisps, blagged from God knows where. Our guests look a little disgruntled. Everyone reassures everyone else that tomorrow will be different because, for the first time, national television will be showcasing the Iceland cricket team.

Television is a big deal. Since Ragnar stopped running the ICA, public engagement has dwindled, through no fault of the cricketers. The truth is, Iceland has never been entirely comfortable with its immigrant population, and their activities rarely garner much media attention (unless they've committed a crime). While native Icelanders were playing cricket, there was a steady level of amused curiosity. When the expats took over, interest dried up. By a lucky twist of fate, though, one of the organisers of the Reykjavík Literary Festival, Halla Oddný Magnúsdóttir, is a television presenter – and she's arranged for both national stations to come to the second game. Tens of thousands of viewers will be introduced to a team they never knew they had; Halla (who has, off her own bat, learned the basics) will interpret the unfamiliar action; Faulks and Holland will give interviews. The publicity will be great.

The Authors are at Kórinn early. They have breakfasted, in the true spirit of the Norse, on the local fauna. Faulks has tried puffin – in its pre-cooked state, the cutest of birds – and is taking some flak from his comrades. At eleven o'clock, the Authors are changed, warmed up, and looking suitably dapper and English for the press. The television people are here, from RÚV and Stöð 2, taking establishing shots and fixing up lights for the coin toss. But the Icelanders are nowhere to be seen.

There's an old saying that if you were to organise a meeting between representatives of England, Germany and Iceland, the English would arrive an hour early, the Germans would be precisely on time, and the Icelanders would turn up when they felt like it. Time is a fluid concept here. The Icelandic attitude to pretty much everything can be summed up by one expression: '*þetta reddast*'. It's the closest thing modern Iceland has to a motto. Very broadly, it means 'it'll be fine', but in a careless, don't-bother-me sort of way. The television people take it all in their stride, and fill time talking to Faulks.

"Icelanders don't understand this game," admits the interviewer. "We have no inkling of what it's about. What is the magic of cricket?"

Faulks says he's not sure he can sum it up in a sentence, "But I suppose if you think of chess as the ultimate board game, and bridge as the ultimate card game, then cricket is the ultimate ball game, since it has so many tactical variations and possibilities."

I doubt any sentence has come closer to the mark.

"Some people get quite obsessed about cricket, don't they?" presses the interviewer.

"I dream about it most nights," says Faulks. "And the things I think about most during the day are death, cricket and sex. Probably in that order."

It is half past eleven. Still no sign of the Iceland team. *Þetta reddast.* The television people fill more time talking to Tom Holland, who has, for the occasion, written a skaldic poem about Faulks:

> In Reykjavík they know his bat,
> The ball-foe, slayer of the puffin,
> Who made the Iceland bowlers
> Food for ravens.

There is a certain degree of artistic licence here, of course. The puffin bit stands up, but 'ball-foe' is doing a lot of work: Faulks scores 0, 4 and 0 on the tour.

It is twelve o'clock. The television people pack up their cameras, without having spoken to a single Icelander. Jakob and Abhi belatedly appear, but the media have departed. I'm frustrated, and can't hide it. The match was supposed to start an hour ago! Didn't they want to be on television?

Þetta reddast, inevitably.

The Authors are better prepared for the second game, and pack their attack with swing bowlers, who make Iceland work hard for their runs. The ringer bowls and fields out of his skin, running Abhi out with a superb pick up and throw. Abhi disputes the dismissal furiously, and stern words are exchanged. Wilson, a man of no nonsense on paper or in deed, is particularly unimpressed. Jakob, once more, arrests Iceland's decline. His unbeaten 18 is the highest score in their 79 for 6. It proves too much for the tourists, who slide from 38 for 2 to 67 all out. Their last three are run out, including Wilson, beaten by a throw from Abhi, who follows up with another crowing celebration.

The tension is now palpable, and Derick does his best to smooth things over before the third game. Iceland have secured the Halldór Laxness Trophy, so Derick sportingly weakens his eleven by resting Chamley and Lakmal, replacing them with me and a young refugee (who later turns out to be a gifted cameraman, and becomes the ICA's official photographer). The Authors bat first this time and are confronted by the lesser threat of Derick opening the bowling with his off-breaks, followed by Leslie – who hardly ever bowls – me, and the refugee.

The pot boils over when Abhi, whom Derick has diplomatically stationed far away, on the deep midwicket boundary, screams a succession of impassioned lbw appeals against Wilson. The batsman matches towards Abhi, pointing his finger and adopting his most headmasterly air.

"That's enough, do you hear me?" barks Wilson. "Enough! If you don't know how to behave, at least shut up." Abhi utters not another word for the rest of the day – not even when I dismiss Wilson. Cook snuffs out three, and the Authors post 118 for 9.

It is hard to expect anyone other than an Englishman to adopt the village-green strategy of winning by the smallest possible margin, but Derick engineers the Icelandic chase expertly. The lesser talents have their chance to bat, and Iceland tiptoe unsteadily towards the target. Lee makes 32, but we go into the last over – bowled by the ringer – needing six to win. Dushan is on strike, and I am at the other end. Twice Dushan turns down a single, twice he swishes at thin air, and twice he hits the stadium roof (no run, and dead ball) going for the winning hit. The result is an unlikely maiden, and a consolation win for the Authors. Their mood improves all the more around midnight when, rolling out of a seafood restaurant in various stages of intoxication, they see the rainclouds briefly part to reveal a small but unmistakable streak of the northern lights.

The third day of the Authors' tour is dedicated to publicity. The television companies have requested an exhibition of cricket outdoors and, though the rain barely abates, a few hardy souls convene at Hljómskálagarðurinn, an ornamental park on the edge of the city centre. Halla is here with the camera crews, and gamely hits a few strokes, as does Vera, the production assistant. And this time, there are Icelanders to thrust in front of the lens. Leslie is a little shy, but Lee – ever the performer – is in his element when asked about the appeal of cricket. "It's better playing with other people than playing with yourself," is his rejoinder, which makes the evening's news. The British ambassador, Michael Nevin, makes an appearance, and turns out to be a capable cricketer.

We're all invited to a reception at the ambassador's house, after which we traipse back across the sodden park to the University of Iceland, where a selection of the Authors are to take part in a question-and-answer session as part of the Reykjavík Literary Festival. This is to take place in the student bar, where a couple of hundred sports fans are celebrating Iceland's 2–0 win over Ukraine, which has kept them on course to reach the football world cup.

We're greeted by the festival's organiser, Stella Soffía Jóhannesdóttir, who is the embodiment of Nordic creativity, charm and charisma. She asks who'd like to join the panel. I've learned that this is a delicate question for the Authors. As a rule, writers don't much like being on panels – especially without the lure of a fee – but Faulks and Holland, as the bestsellers, are always in demand. They've already done television, though, and it might be time to shove someone else into the limelight. But Stella proves irresistible and is overwhelmed with offers.

The enthusiastic volunteers balk a little when she outlines the topics for discussion. The first (the history and raison d'être of the Authors' team) poses no problems, but the second (cricket's appearances in English literature) elicits worried glances. There aren't many examples. Charles Dickens's *The Pickwick Papers* recounts a match, and Catherine Morland is described as enjoying cricket in Jane Austen's *Northanger Abbey*, but that's about it for the big-name writers. There's a lengthy account of a game in A. G. Macdonnell's *England, Their England*, in which the author takes half a dozen pages over a hilarious description of a catch being taken, but they can't *all* talk about that.

Stella then introduces the host, a stout, twinkly-eyed man with thick spectacles and wild beard. She tells us he has played cricket for some years, so will know the right questions to ask.

"Well, you know, that is not quite correct," he says, with a historian's pedantry.

It is Stefán Pálsson.

"I thought you played cricket for Iceland?" Stella asks.

"Well, perhaps you and I would call it cricket. I doubt if these gentlemen would recognise what we were doing," responds Stefán. "But we'll see if we can find an approach that works."

The approach turns out to be Stefán pacing to stage left and right, microphone in hand, in front of a row of bemused English writers. Never lost for words, his loquacity – fuelled by the presence of an audience and a steady supply of beer – reaches new heights. Occasionally Campbell says a few words about the origins of his team, Wilson briefly draws a footballing analogy, or McGowan makes a witty remark, but the show is most definitely Stefán's. He rambles on about wrestling, the old dirt sports ground at Melavöllur, and the recent history of the Left-Green Movement in Iceland, babbling away with increasing boozy fuzziness until he takes one pace too many and falls off the stage. The Authors look at each other. Stella buries her face in her hands.

The press coverage, when the Authors return to the UK, is substantial. They have given a great deal of time and publicity to Icelandic cricket, generating media interest in Iceland and overseas, and stimulating curiosity around the world. It seems like a flash in the pan – but turns out to be proof of concept.

While the Authors are on stage at the university, Iceland's cricketers are at the international airport, en route to Prague for a second attempt at the Pepsi Cup. David and Leslie are again unable to travel, as is Prabhath, but Nolan has stepped in, thus strengthening the seam attack. And there is a bonus, in the form of the reappearance of Sammy. After nearly a decade in Norway, he and his family have decided to move back to Iceland – and this homecoming apparently begins with a week-long cricket tour. Sammy's wife is a very tolerant woman.

History repeats itself in the group stage: Iceland manage two wins, one against Winterthur. But a very strong academy team, from Faridabad in India, lays waste to all comers, and Iceland find themselves in the fifth-place play-off again. Their prospects of equalling the previous year's achievement look good when their opponents – a team from Dubai – slump to 94 for 6 in pursuit of 160.

Derick has enjoyed a fine tournament, as a batsman (with 293 runs in five innings, including 132, a new record for an Icelander) and as captain. But his decision to bowl himself, with 24 needed from the final over, is bold in the extreme. He has three seamers at his disposal – Dushan, Lakmal and Abhi – but stakes the game on his own off-spin.

There's a thin line between brave and foolhardy. Derick has a lovely technique as a slow bowler but, as he learned at Eton, spinners ain't for the death. He has only bowled a couple of overs in the tournament, so this is a huge gamble. And it doesn't pay off: he's hit for four sixes. The fallout is nuclear. Some of the Icelanders defend Derick's courage; others deride his decision as reckless. The rancour accompanies the team back to Reykjavík. Strong words are said. The mood is so bad that few feel like practising during the off-season, let alone playing.

The winter is long. For my part, I had gone to London shortly after the Authors tour and have no inkling that something's amiss. It's not until I start fielding requests from touring teams, wanting to visit Iceland in 2018, that I call Abhi.

I hear a dejected voice.

"Mate, I can't even tell you what happened. It looks bad," he sighs.

I attempt reassurance.

"I'm sure it will have blown over by next season."

"Next season? I don't think there will be another season."

I've never heard Abhi talk like this. Abhi is an optimist. If you tell him a meteorite is heading for the Earth, he will try and arrange one last cricket practice.

"Just give people time," I say.

Abhi sighs again. "It has already been three months. Everyone's crazy with everyone else. Nothing's happening. Honestly, mate. I think it's over."

It's dismaying news. Everyone has worked so hard – Ragnar, Abhi, everyone. Things seem to work out, chaotically at the best of times but, you know, *þetta reddast*. It can't just end.

I ask if there's anything I can do.

VIII

VIRAL

> While the English Cricket Board is fretting over the details of
> its new 100-ball competition, the Icelandic Cricket Association
> announced it would get the jump on England and host their
> own Hundred match, at which point, presumably, all of Britain's
> mothers and children leapt with joy and booked their tickets to
> Iceland immediately, unable to resist the new format's charm.
>
> Fidel Fernando, ESPN Cricinfo, 2018

I'm not sure Jakob and Abhi know what they're in for. They're grateful for my offer of help but, while they're hoping for the survival of cricket in Iceland, my ambition is growth. Rapid growth. My approach to getting things done is, for want of a better expression, an acquired taste. I settle on plans quickly, and don't like to sit through hours of turgid committee-room negotiation. Do we all agree my idea is a good idea? Yes. Shall I do it, then? Yes. That's my kind of meeting. Jakob is the most easy-going chairman imaginable and says I can go ahead and do anything that'll help Iceland cricket. Abhi is pleased to be relieved of his burden – he has a plan to make his fortune with a website, of his own devising, which will allow users to create a graphic of their fantasy sports team. How it will earn him a penny is anyone's guess (spoiler alert: it doesn't).

It is January 2018. I take a piece of notepaper and sketch out some thoughts.

Our assets
1. We have had 126 players, including 80 who have played in a representative Iceland team, and 55 native Icelanders.
2. Jakob is an ideal figurehead as chairman.
3. Abhi has a lot of energy.
4. Derick has learned quickly as captain.

5. Nolan has a lot of cricketing expertise. Keenan has an excellent technique. Lee is a gifted communicator and great with children. They would make decent coaches.
6. The Sri Lankans are brilliant at hospitality. Dushan and Lakmal are bakers, Sadun is a talented cook, Prabhath works in tourism and Chamley's cousin has a car hire company.
7. Sammy's back and is one of the original players. He might help us get a link back to them.
8. Leslie has a good brain for business and loads of contacts at venues in Reykjavík.
9. David is as smart as a fox, and meticulous.

Our liabilities
1. We have just 24 active players. We have not put out two full teams for a domestic match since 2008.
2. We have undertaken three tours, but only played against clubs.
3. We are 18 seasons old but are still yet to play another national team.
4. We have Twitter but only 218 followers. We have posted seven times in two years.
5. We get little press attention. Few people outside Iceland know we have a team.
6. We have no savings, and no income.
7. We don't have an eye-catching identity to attract an influx of new players and supporters.
8. We don't have a ground. We've attempted to play on grass at five venues but with little success. We now play on a lethal artificial football pitch in a sports stadium.

My immediate thought is that we should run another summer tour to the UK, in a different mould from the last. Whereas 2017's trip was essentially a social one, forming part of an English cricket club's festival to support their fundraising, the 2018 tour would promote us, not our hosts. And instead of playing clubs, we'd find oppositions with public standing, to lend our matches prominence. I try to convince Jakob of all this.

"Our opening match should be against the MCC," I begin.

"Right, okay, great," Jakob says. "What's the MCC?"

This will take more explaining than I thought.

"It's the most famous cricket club in the world. Their home ground is Lord's."

"Great. So we'll play at Lord's?"

"Well, no, probably not Lord's. They hosted Afghanistan at Lord's on their first tour to England. But they might host us somewhere smaller. A nice village ground, perhaps."

"Sounds good."

"And we should play the Club Cricket Conference."

"Okay. Who are they?"

"It's an organisation that represents amateur cricket. Their team is basically the best English players without professional contracts."

"Sounds good."

"And we should play the Authors."

"The guys from last year? Didn't they get really pissed off with Abhi?" There is a hint of uncertainty in Jakob's tone.

"Yup, that's them. They have a big following, which will be good for publicity. And we'll tell them it's their chance to level the series."

"Sounds good."

"And then we'll play Switzerland."

"Wait. Switzerland? The national team?"

"The national team."

Jakob pauses for a moment.

"They play cricket in Switzerland?"

"We play cricket in *Iceland*, Jakob."

"Fair enough."

The green light having been given, I enter travel agent mode and begin organising the tour, while Abhi does his best to shake the players out of their high dudgeon and hibernation. It takes a while to ease tensions and smooth brows, but the news of the tour perks everyone up. It's even agreed that we'll start a fourth indoor series between Reykjavík and Kópavogur. I have the idea of naming this rivalry the Volcanic Ashes, and design a fitting trophy: a replica Ashes urn, bearing an Icelandic adaptation of the poem published by *Melbourne Punch* to commemorate England's original success, in Australia in 1883:

Er Ragnar heim kemur með kerið, með kerið
Þið knattleikinn after umberið, umberið
Valhöll mun hringja hátt
og heimamenn fagna dátt
Að sjá Ragnar heimkominn með kerið, med kerið
Og komu alls liðsins með kerið

When Ragnar comes home with the urn, the urn
Knattleikr will thereby return, return
Valhalla will ring loud
The people will feel proud
To see Ragnar come home with the urn, the urn
And the rest coming home with the urn

The urn is set in a base of Icelandic volcanic basalt, and suitably filled: with ashes from all five eruptions in Iceland since the formation of the ICA. It's an impressive trophy, not quite befitting a less-than-11-a-side cricket series played on an indoor football pitch in the suburbs of Reykjavík.

We decide to stage the first two Volcanic Ashes matches before the summer season, and the last three after it. I'm put in charge of arranging them and have success at the first attempt: 22 players enlist. A dozen new faces appear, the most since the original Icelanders were running the show. It seems a good omen.

A little into April, I cross my fingers and send out a press release, with details of our English tour. The BBC picks it up, quoting Jakob, and even adding a couple of lines reporting on the second Volcanic Ashes match. It's our first BBC coverage for 15 years.

I haven't used Twitter before but feel I ought to have a stab at it, and Jakob digs out the password. My first few tweets are about our fixtures in England. We are to play the MCC in Hampton Hill, and I note that its population of 19,372 would make it the fourth largest city in Iceland. The Hampton Hill residents' association replies, insisting they're a village – a claim I repudiate, pointing out that the residents' association alone has enough Twitter followers to make it Iceland's tenth largest city. The tweet garners 45 likes. Well, it's a start.

I adopt a 'voice' for Twitter – one I think best suits an Icelandic sporting organisation. We are, by virtue of having never played another country, the worst national team in the world. We can only look up at our betters. But that is not very Icelandic. It would be more apt, I reason, to be the glorious upstart, brimming with misplaced self-confidence, and ready to 'punch up'.

This is the persona I adopt when I tweet that Iceland's contribution to world history is the discovery of Greenland, Canada and the USA, whereas Switzerland's contribution is the Toblerone bar, available at all airports. There is, in Twitter terms, a titter. The public seem to like it. We gain a dozen followers. A kitchen showroom in Hampton Hill offers us £100 as sponsorship, and a light goes on (in my head, not in the kitchen showroom).

I ask Jakob if we have ever tried crowdfunding. He says we haven't, but Lee once raised a tidy sum to buy a big top for Sirkus Íslands. I decide to see if we can raise £1,000 to help with the tour and set up a donations page.

> Can't afford to buy your own IPL franchise? Then become a part-owner of the newest international cricket team. A donation of £50 makes you a patron of Icelandic cricket. Our success is yours!

Almost immediately, I receive an email from a man called Sidhant Garg, who is the moderator of the cricket forum on Reddit. The online community, he says, has been captivated by the thought of supporting the world's smallest national team. They've had enough of the 'Big Three' – Australia, England and India – attracting all the money and attention, and they'd like to do something symbolic. We agree that if he can raise £3,000 (a ludicrous amount, it seems to me), the members of his cricket forum – all 60,000 of them – will become the collective sponsors of the Iceland team for 2018 and 2019.

Sidhant's community raises the money in a matter of days. Crowdfunding donations, meanwhile, are approaching £5,000. It's more than the ICA's total sponsorship income over the last two decades. And it's far more than we need to get the tour underway. Jakob and I agree to ring-fence the £3,000 from Reddit for a children's cricket programme. The BBC reports on our windfall, as does Cricket Australia. We reach 500 followers on Twitter – more than double what we had a fortnight previously.

I spend an evening looking up national cricket teams on Twitter. In terms of followers, we're not even in the top 100. There are teams who've never tweeted, yet have more followers than us. The really organised amateur national teams have 10,000. The professional ones, who pay their players and sometimes get to the World Cup, have at least 20,000. That, I figure, is where we want to be: the most-followed amateur cricket team in the world. Hell, we could even call ourselves the most popular.

It appears our recent boost has put us above Greece, and I decide to treat it like a campaign, taking on a country at a time. I try to be humorous, but merciless.

> Thank you all for helping us get past Greece in the Twitter followers table. Next up is Saudi Arabia, who haven't tweeted for six years. We need to get past them before they remember their Twitter password.

> Next up is Brazil. Let's inflict on them their worst international sporting defeat. Well, maybe not their worst. Their second worst. #Brazil1Germany7

> Vladimir Putin can ride horses, fly planes, wrestle bears, eat bricks, fart the national anthem and shoot the moon through a basketball hoop. One day he might even win an election without imprisoning the opposition. Let's take on Russia.

People start doubting that this is real. That is, a real cricket association behind a real cricket team playing real cricket in real life. The general view is that it's all a hoax. No proper team would address other teams with such impertinence. But people are taking notice.

I have a brief spat with a Twitter user who's outraged that all our present players are expats. I indulge myself in a robust defence of immigration, which is picked up by a South African news organisation. Jakob and I agree to introduce an award, named after our xenophobic interlocutor, for our immigrant player of the year.

117

We pass 1,000 followers, but Russia are still some way ahead of us.

> We've asked you to help us overtake Russia. Several of you have seemed hesitant and advised caution. Get a grip. What's the worst that can happen? It's not as if they can just come over to your country and kill you while you sit at home using Twi

That wakes them up. Cricket Russia takes to Twitter – the first team to take us on in similar vein. Emboldened, I push the envelope.

> We see that Cricket Russia have returned from their three year break photocopying ballot papers. And they want to send us a present. How nice! Here's the address to send it to: Denmark Cricket Board, Bacon House, Legoland Lane, Denmark.

I create a note of attempted delivery – the ones couriers leave when you're not at home – to suggest the Russian 'present' has arrived.

> You were out when we attempted delivery.
> We have:
> - ☐ Left it with your neighbour
> - ☐ Returned it to your local delivery office
> - ☐ Dissolved it in your next cup of tea
> - ☐ Hidden it in the tip of an umbrella
> - ☑ Smeared it over your front door handle
> - ☐ Decided to make it look like suicide

Russia falls that evening. The USA follows next morning. We pass 2,000 followers. Also biting the bait are ESPN, who ask for an interview, which they publish in the form of a text message conversation. One of the questions asks whether we watch the HBO series *Game of Thrones* in Iceland. I respond that we don't, because we "live it every day", adding that "when we get home from work we just want to crack open a beer, put our feet up and catch up with *Yeh Rishta Kya Kehlata Hai* like every other Icelander". Now, just to be clear, Hindi soap operas are not broadcast on Icelandic television. But my remark precipitates a deluge of likes, comments and enquiries from Indian fans, agog with surprise to learn that cricket is played in Iceland (and that we follow the dramatic lives of the much-put-upon Singhania family).

Another moment of whimsy provides a further boost to our burgeoning fame on Twitter. Ireland are about to play their very first Test match, against Pakistan in Dublin. Ireland's big moment seems a perfect opportunity for a misunderstanding – Iceland is, after all, only one consonant away.

> Kits ironed. Bags packed. Anti potato famine inoculations up to date. We've boarded our biggest ship [photograph of Cod War era coastguard vessel inserted here] and we're off to Malahide. Góðan dag Pakistan! So excited for this. Such an amazing time for us. Wish us luck!

The forecast for Dublin is 9°C, with light rain and 25 mph winds.

> Arrived in Dublin. Oh boy. We totally misjudged how long we would need to adjust to this climate. Exhausted. Half the team has heatstroke. Send us rehydration packs.

This amuses the Pakistan fans, who have otherwise been a bit grumpy: Fawad Alam, a fine player who has enjoyed a formidable start to his international career, has been left out of the team in favour of the chief selector's nephew – an inferior player. I post a list of the Iceland and Pakistan teams on Twitter; my Pakistan eleven include the chief selector's nephew, niece, best friend and bicycle. The tweet goes viral. The following day, I announce that Fawad Alam has been granted Icelandic citizenship and will be playing for us. Various Pakistani news outlets report the story, with tongue in cheek. A few less humorously minded Twitter users tell us Pakistan are playing Ireland, not Iceland. I address them en masse.

> Can't you read? Look at the ICC press release! Do you really think we'd have come all the way to Dublin if we didn't have an important first ever Test match tomorrow?

Our following surpasses Bermuda who, like the USA, have played in the World Cup. We are doing well.

Meanwhile, back at home, Abhi has been putting together proposals for expanding our domestic cricket. He suggests an outdoor six-a-side competition, featuring Reykjavík and Kópavogur, plus three other teams. I suggest we call them Hafnarfjörður, Garðabær and Seltjarnarnes, the other towns in the capital area. They could provide the basis of new clubs, playing full cricket matches, outdoors, in the T20 and T10 formats. We could even establish our own outdoor ground, to be the home of Icelandic cricket. Abhi tells me not to think too big too soon.

I turn to Twitter for team nicknames, and the polls come up with Hafnarfjörður Hammers, Garðabær Geysirs and Seltjarnarnes Sunsets. An Indian company called Influx Worldwide offers us a free graphic design service, and before long we have a full suite of beautiful, professionally produced logos: five for the domestic teams, one for the Volcanic Ashes, and three for proposed competitions. I suggest we hold the six-a-side competition on the longest day of the summer, when we have round-the-clock daylight, and call it the Summer Solstice Sixes. David comes up with Sixty Ball Shootout for a T10 contest. And I devise the conceit of mimicking the Indian Premier League – now the world's most popular and profitable cricket tournament – by calling our T20 competition the Íslensk Premier League. From the IPL to the ÍPL (pronounced "ee-pee-ell", as I repeatedly take pains to explain on Twitter, as the Indian fans respond with a mixture of outrage and delight).

The ICA gets its own logo, too: a shield showing a cricket ball becoming a gyrfalcon (Iceland's national bird). It's clean and attractive – and a lot more elegant than the logo I'd hastily created for the caps the previous summer. It inspires us to give our national side its own nickname: the Falcons (with apologies to the Atlanta football team).

There are new jerseys for all the teams. I insist on a centralised design approach. This is the only way to 'do' jerseys, in my view. When coloured clothing came to the World Cup in 1992, each team was designated a different colour, and there was a consistency of appearance; it's widely acknowledged to be the best World Cup kit cricket ever had. The same approach was adopted for the English counties in 1993 – and the same nostalgia is felt for those original designs. The trouble is, as soon as you allow teams to do their own thing, three quarters of them end up playing in blue, and the rest in red.

Our designers incorporate the swooping gyrfalcon into a new national team jersey, on which the Reddit cricket community are to add their own logo and slogan. Sidhant has put together a shortlist of eight suggestions put forward by the forum. 'Ice Garry' appears to be a play on Australian wicketkeeper Brad Haddin's exhortation to spin bowler Nathan 'Garry' Lyon. 'Peter Borren for President' puts a relatively unremarkable Dutch cricketer front and centre. 'Willing Flustered Cockroach' and 'Wan Physical Goose' go over my head completely, and I begin to regret promising the Redditors they can choose any slogan they want. Are we about to go the same way as the UK's National Oceanography Centre, forced to name its new submarine 'Boaty McBoatface' after a similar poll? Or the same way as the Solid Waste Department of Austin, Texas, which the public chose to rename 'The Fred Durst Society of the Humanities and Arts'? Or Mountain Dew, whose survey determined that their new apple-flavour drink should be called 'Hitler Did Nothing Wrong'?

Sure enough, 'Crickety McCricketface' is on the shortlist. 'Legalise Sandpaper' is a little more on point, relating to the Australian ball-tampering scandal the previous March. 'ICC #PigThree' is apparently a dig at the richest cricket boards, which might not be especially tactful, given we're about to tour England. The final suggestion is 'Grow the Game', which conveys a similar sentiment more positively, and is my favourite. Sidhant says it's his favourite, too – and mercifully, it wins the vote.

Sidhant tells me a logo has already been designed, which is faintly terrifying news, but it turns out to be a masterpiece. It depicts Yggdrasill, a sacred tree in Norse mythology: its roots connect with history, life and the elements, and its branches extend to the heavens.

In Reykjavík, Jakob has been working hard to bring more refugees to the cricket family. He establishes a direct link with the Reykjavík City Council, who encourage new arrivals from Afghanistan to join us, and even pay for their cricket equipment. SBS World News send a crew from Australia to discuss asylum in Iceland, so Jakob, Abhi and three refugees hit a ball around in front of the parliament building, for the cameras.

The inaugural Summer Solstice Sixes begin well. It's cold, but dry. Lakmal and Dushan hit the ball everywhere. Derick plays with his usual street-smarts and stealth. I captain Reykjavík to fourth place, and though I deploy the standard six-a-side field, placing a man on each corner of the Kórinn football pitch, I cop an earful for "bad captaincy" from an English teenager who is making his first (and last) appearance in an Icelandic game. He cops an earful back. We only beat Seltjarnarnes, who are a bit of a let-down, not least when – after losing their third game on the trot – they go home, claiming they are too tired to continue. Abhi, captaining Kópavogur, engages in 15 minutes of histrionics over a disputed dismissal, and for a moment it looks as though this is a terminal blow to the tournament – but his team-mates manage to drag him back from the brink, and the cricket restarts. Derick leads Garðabær, unbeaten, to the final against Hafnarfjörður, led by Sadun. But there is a problem. Sadun, in dropping a high catch, has hurt his finger, and insists that the final be postponed until it feels better. A month, he suggests. He may be bad at fielding – and at coping with pain – but he is nevertheless a fearsome bowler and even more terrifying when angered, so everybody agrees to put the final off until we get back from England.

After the Sixes, Derick posts a few videos on our chat group, one of which shows me bowling an over against Kópavogur, which – conceited fellow that I am – delights me. The subsequent online chat is a microcosm of Icelandic cricket.

Kit: The thing I like best about the video is that I bowl
        six balls: 200404. Lee then says "10 off the over, that's
        better" and then Abhi, as scorer, calls to the umpires
        "One to go! One to go!" And his scorecard shows that
        my over was hit for 13.

Abhi: Please don't start an argument here mate. Every over
        scorecard was updated.

Kit: Only you would watch a video of 10 runs being scored
        off six balls and still insist you'd watched 13 being
        scored off five.

Lee: Only you would watch a video of six balls being
         bowled by you.

Our Twitter following is well past 5,000 by mid-June, and I'm
keen to keep trying anything for attention before we go on tour. In
particular, I want to stir things up in the UK as best I can, ready for
our arrival.

> Time for another Twitter followers battle. Next up is Guernsey.
> Kind of similar to us but more boring. We both have cows but
> we invented skyr whereas they went no further than cream. We
> both have traditional wool sweaters but ours is more interesting
> and harder to knit.

Guernsey actually engages, albeit briefly. "Always ready to defend
our beaches," comes the reply. I can't resist suggesting that the
history books suggest otherwise. Guernsey makes no further attempt
to fight (no, don't go there, come on, we're bigger than that, aren't
we?). So on I blithely go.

> Don't visit the glacier caves of Iceland. Visit Guernsey and see
> its concrete towers, which were built in 1778, and were used as
> concrete towers, with the aim of stopping anyone coming to
> Guernsey who didn't love concrete towers. A purpose they still
> fulfil to this very day.

In another couple of weeks, such bons mots have seen off not
only Guernsey, but also Gibraltar ("all you've got is a rock"), Sweden
("if you've ever waited in all day for an Ikea delivery, you'll have
wondered what it might be like to hit a Swedish person on the head
with a cricket bat"), and Denmark ("let's overtake them while they're
distracted by an important task at head office: they're looking for
a slightly orangey one with four nobbly bits and a sort of lump on
the end", followed by a picture of eight adults playing with Lego).
The next team we need to defeat in a Twitter followers battle is
Switzerland – which is apt, given that we will soon face them on the
cricket field.

IX

INTERNATIONALS

I mean, look. Joking aside. An Icelandic national cricket team.
Come on. It's a hoax, right? It has to be a hoax.

Jonathan Agnew, BBC *Test Match Special*, 2018

It's a strange feeling being a Londoner visiting London in the guise
of a tourist. I was born in the capital, and have lived there most of
my life, but now I must encounter it with fresh eyes, as the innocent
abroad. I am now widely referred to as the "Iceland Cricket Twitter
guy", my real identity still a secret. So in the spirit of the enterprise,
I post wide-eyed comments describing my first encounters with
McDonalds, Harry Potter and trains – none of which exist in Iceland.

I'm on my way to Leeds, in Yorkshire, where England are playing
India. A little more than a year has passed since Abhi and I first
met, when I tentatively suggested I might be able to get Icelandic
cricket onto the BBC. And now, at Headingley stadium, I'm to be
interviewed live on *Test Match Special*. It's the most famous cricket
show in the world, has been broadcasting since 1957, and is home
to commentators who have been calling the game for longer than
I've been following cricket. Jonathan Agnew, the BBC's cricket
correspondent since 1991, will be interviewing me. Within a few
moments of arriving at the ground, I am introduced to former
international stars like Mike Atherton, Harbhajan Singh and Michael
Vaughan. By the time I'm ushered into a chair alongside the great
Agnew, I'm a little lost for words. I try to assume the chutzpah by
now expected of the ICA – of which I am now *de facto* secretary
– but I'm floored by Agnew persistently pressing me to admit the
whole thing's a hoax.

The irony is that, had he asked this question 18 years ago, the
answer would have been an honest and resounding "yes".

All *Test Match Special* devotees know that the programme has
an enduring association with cake. Guests and listeners have been

124

bringing cakes to the commentary box for decades. Even Queen Elizabeth sent one in, to celebrate the show's anniversary (or her anniversary; I can't remember, and in any case they'd both been around for absolutely ages). My offering is six *hjónabandssælur* ('happy marriage cakes') which are about as traditional as Icelandic cakes get – oaty, jammy and practically indestructible.

It's all good publicity for the tour, which is just as well, because there are some teething problems. I return to Iceland for a series of pre-tour training sessions with the squad. Abhi has, to save money, decided against booking Kórinn, so musters everybody at a sports facility round the corner from his apartment in Kópavogur. There are two big playing fields of artificial grass – but both are full of footballers. Abhi appears and tells us he hasn't booked anything, but it's fine, because we can practise on the asphalt tennis court.

I don't know how other national cricket teams prepared for their first international match, but I'm willing to bet they didn't train with a tennis ball, or on a tennis court. I have flown back to Iceland for this. A kit bag is upended and propped against a fence. Another bag is placed about ten metres away. We are going to play tapeball, without the tape. There is no warm-up, no catching practice, no structure. Derick is out first ball: everybody yells in jubilation, Derick is relieved of the bat, and that's *his* pre-tour batting done. It is utterly pointless – and the following day, I remonstrate with Abhi. He protests that it is all part of the plan.

"Have you played on the artificial grass? The bounce is not right for the UK. We need to practise on fast pitches."

I ask why we don't play all our matches on ten-metre stretches of asphalt, if they're so much better.

"Concrete is good for UK pitches. Artificial grass the ball holds for a second."

I try to keep calm, but fail.

"Abhi, you are being totally stupid. Nobody *in the world* practises on a hard tennis court."

"It was always my plan to practise there. We need to practise on fast pitches."

Switzerland are going to destroy us.

The situation gets worse. In the days before departure, Keenan's leave is cancelled by his boss, who wants to go on holiday himself.

And Chamley's visa has, for the second year running, failed to come through. We are down to twelve players. In Keenan, we've lost a batter and spinner; in Chamley, we've lost our back-up wicketkeeper. I am drafted in as a replacement spinner, and Alex Sabelli, an Italian friend of Jakob and Lee's, is brought in to bat and keep wicket.

Jakob, Abhi and I go to London ahead of the main group to make sure things are in order, and to have a meeting with Darren Talbot, an English coach who runs a successful cricket academy, and has been providing advice from a distance. He has volunteered to sacrifice a week of work to coach the Iceland team in England. A veteran of the Surrey circuit, he has abundant experience of top-level amateur cricket, and clear ideas about how the Iceland team should approach their tour. He is amused to learn of the tennis court debacle and assures us that everything will be different when the players arrive in London.

On the eve of the tour, Jakob, Abhi and I play for my Sunday team, the Adhocs, which I have captained for a couple of decades. Leslie, who has been in the UK visiting friends, brings the Icelandic contingent up to four. Abhi bowls wonderfully, but Jakob and I are rusty. When our turn comes to bat, we manage eight runs between us, and Leslie sprains his ankle. It is an inauspicious start.

The rest of the squad arrives on Monday morning, and squeezes into a squalid Travelodge in Kingston-upon-Thames. It is a horrible hotel and, as the tour manager and travel agent, I shoulder the blame. Sadun suggests I make amends by providing the team with weed and hookers, but I slink away with David, Jakob, and my small daughter Astrid, to make a radio appearance on Talksport. I stay in the production box, trying to distract Astrid from discovering that buttons and faders on a mixing desk are fun to play with, while Jakob and David assume their on-air roles. Jakob is there as chairman, to play the part of inspirational, aspirational figurehead. David is there to give the listeners someone to relate to: a dry, realistic Englishman. Their answer to the final question is typical. "So, will you beat Switzerland?" Jakob gives the Icelander's answer. "Yeah, of course." David is more English about it. "No."

Tuesday dawns bright and warm – too warm, really, for Icelandic cricketers, even those of Asian descent. Everyone is used to the

Arctic, and it's well over 25°C in Kingston. Our match against the MCC is at Hampton Hill, in one of the Royal Parks. This means deer roam about freely, paying little heed to tourists, cricketing or otherwise. We have a photo call at the kitchen showroom, where we pose among the appliances, wearing our Iceland jerseys and deadpan expressions.

Darren and Derick have imposed a strict call time, and everyone passes muster except Leslie, whose ankle turns out to be badly sprained, ruling him out of the week's cricket, and Sadun, who's decided a late breakfast trumps minutiae like briefings and warm-ups. Bushy Park is as pretty as a picture, and Hampton Hill are outgoing hosts. The whole club seems to have turned out to watch. Several spectators are wearing replica Iceland cricket jerseys, which we had given to our principal supporters and sponsors. The BBC have sent the producer of their *Stumped* podcast to cover the game, so I grab Sammy and tell him to summarise the last fifteen years of Iceland cricket for them. He looks hesitant – Sammy is a man for whom remembering what he had for lunch requires a herculean effort. A commentary team from Guerilla Cricket, an online cricket channel, has also come for the match. I provide them with the services of Nolan, who has the smoothest vibe and deepest voice (save for Sadun, but there's no way I'm putting him on air, and he hasn't turned up yet anyway). The whole scene is idyllic. The captains go out to toss. Deer lope across the outfield. The club barmaid, Lucy – an athletic blonde in a tartan miniskirt – brings our players a drink. One or two gaze longingly at her. Darren tries to focus their attention on the game.

I am to sit out the first game, as is Lee: our first-choice wicketkeeper must be kept fresh for the greater battles to come. Darren decides to field all seven of our front-line bowlers, and they have their work cut out, as the MCC make a rapid start on a lightning outfield. Sadun, in spite of his breakfast ballast, bowls with pace, taking two wickets. Dushan pulls off a wonderful catch to dismiss one of the openers, but after these early fillips, we begin to wilt. Nolan finds bounce, but is tamed; Lakmal can find no seam movement and Dushan no swing. Derick turns to spin, and though he and Prabhath extract turn from the dry surface, they too are quickly mastered. Only Abhi, with his fussy variations, has any luck, taking two wickets late in the innings. The declaration comes after two and a half hours, setting Iceland 236 to win from 52 overs.

It is a generous target, but the injury to Leslie, alongside the absences of Keenan and Chamley, has left holes in our top six. For a start, there is no obvious opening partnership. Realising he has three chances, before the Switzerland game, to find a combination that works, Darren decides to drop Derick to three, promote Lakmal into the top six, and experiment at the top. David, who scored a century opening the batting at Kórinn three years previously, is a sensible choice; Abhi is not, but brightens on hearing Darren's instruction to "get into their heads".

Alas, it does not go well. Abhi is dismissed almost immediately, and David does not last much longer. Lakmal prods and pokes for a quarter of an hour before being dismissed for a 15-ball duck. But, from 20 for 3, we are rescued by the ever-reliable Derick and Dushan, who advance the score to 100 in a flurry of enterprising strokes. Both pass 50, and for a moment we threaten to pull off an upset – but only for a moment. Derick and Dushan are outfoxed by spin, and the middle order of Alex, Sammy and Jakob muster just 10 between them. Our collapse is dramatic and emphatic: the last seven fall for 37 runs; the last four without addition to the score.

Even so, the mood after the game is bright. The MCC captain and Hampton Hill committee present various awards, and there are speeches and kind words of greeting, thankfully received by the Icelanders. MCC teams are good at this sort of thing. They see themselves, not without reason, as the diplomatic service of English cricket. From Afghanistan at Lord's, down to Iceland among the deer, they want to be the ones doing the welcoming. There is but one elephant in the room: they have given us a sporting target to chase, and we have missed it by miles. It will only get harder from here.

If you're male and considered good enough to play as a full-time professional cricketer in England, you're signed by one of the 18 counties and earn your keep as a sportsman. If you're not quite good enough – or striving to be noticed – you play the highest level of amateur club cricket, and wait to be spotted, or recalled. The Club Cricket Conference, founded in 1915, has waved the flag for the amateur game for over a century. Its influence has waned in recent decades, but it still puts together representative teams to play exhibition matches. Some of these are against the counties' second elevens, providing players with a chance to show their skills in front of those who might be inclined to offer them a contract. Others are against worthy opponents, such as the armed forces, the police – or Iceland.

We play the Club Cricket Conference in a T20 game on Wednesday evening at Hampton Wick, on the other side of Bushy Park. Though the match lacks the prestige of the MCC fixture, everything else points to us being fish out of water. For a start, there are no spectators, and no hospitality. While Hampton Hill treated our visit as a special day for their club, encouraging its members and families to attend, Hampton Wick consider our match to be a ground hiring, and nothing more. The place is deserted, the temperature soaring, and the opposition dangerously proficient. All are top-tier club cricketers; four have been full-time professionals (two in England, one in South Africa, and one in Bangladesh).

Their manager – the fact that they have a manager is another ominous portent – tells Darren we can rotate our entire squad through the game, though Nolan, with his sore shoulder, joins Leslie on the injury list. That means Lee is in, and so am I. We field first again, and the Conference team immediately sprint out of sight. They rack up 200, and though our seamers – Sadun, Dushan, Lakmal and Abhi – bowl heroically, our slow bowlers are annihilated. Neither David, Prabhath nor I are able to keep the scoring below two runs a ball, and several catches are put down. David drops one off me that goes so high, the batters have begun a third run by the time the ball ricochets off his hand and over the boundary for six. The high point comes when Lakmal bowls Ben Compton – grandson of an England great, and soon to be an England prospect himself – neck and crop for 39.

Darren shuffles his batting deck again and decides to try Alex and Prabhath in the top three. Alex does a sterling job, top-scoring with 28, but Darren's insistence that Prabhath has the technique to bat high in the order seems woefully wide of the mark, as he gropes around blindly for four singles. Even Derick and Dushan struggle as David Burton, a fast bowler who has played county cricket for Gloucestershire, Middlesex and Northamptonshire, rattles through his four overs at a cost of just seven runs. We opt for survival, and crawl to 91 for 7 in our 20 overs. It is an education – and a chastening one at that.

Thursday is one of the hottest days ever recorded in London. The mercury has hit 36°C by the time we assemble at the Bank of England's majestic sports ground in Roehampton. Our opponents are the Authors, keen to avenge their defeats in Iceland – and, it soon turns out, a little else besides. The Authors are no prouder, as a cricket team, than any other. They take themselves, on balance, a touch more seriously than the average social team, but are always ready with a handshake or a few kind words. If anything, they're more sensitive about their writing. I played against them, years ago, in a village match in Oxfordshire. One of our batters hit a ball, from Nick Hogg, very hard in the direction of Tom Holland, who tried – and failed – to stop it with his foot.

"Use your hands!" cried Hogg.

"These hands," yelled Holland, "wrote *Rubicon!*"

I am very fond of the Authors and am looking forward to seeing them all again. But when they arrive the handshakes seem firmer than usual and the kind words are spoken through gritted teeth. It transpires that the fixture has assumed the air of a grudge match: the Authors do not have as happy memories of their Icelandic series as I do, and the fracas with Abhi has a lot to do with it. They mean business, and have strengthened their team with magazine editor Phil Walker, and the award-winning writer Richard Beard, both excellent cricketers. The ringer is here, too. Derick loses the toss, and we are consigned to a long, hot afternoon in the field. Beard makes a sublime century, the ringer contributes a powerful 77, and the Authors rack up 251. I have a miserable time with the ball. I bowl two no-more-than-adequate overs and am removed from the attack. I enquire why and am told peremptorily that it's because I've just been hit for six, which is a bit harsh, because I haven't. I later regret complaining, after I am brought back to bowl in the final overs and get massacred. Derick really does need to get over his habit of using spinners at the death.

Darren, still undecided as to the best batting order, tries a third opening combination in as many games. This time it is Alex and Abhi, who do reasonably well, and after both are dismissed, Derick and Dushan bring us up to 109 in mere moments. Just as we are starting to feel optimistic, we lose Derick, Dushan and Sammy in quick succession. When Lakmal falls at 158, Darren gives the order to "go for a good total" rather than aim for victory. The Authors, realising they are destined to win, summon a little sympathy and give the cricket writer Jon Hotten – a good batsman, but by no means a bowler – a couple of overs. Prabhath and Jakob make hay for a while, and we finish only 20 runs short.

Friday is a cricket-free day, and we're invited to a reception at the Embassy of Iceland. Posing for a group photograph in our official tour shirts (all except Sadun, who has something better to do) and listening to a message of welcome from the chargé d'affaires, Þurý Björk Björgvinsdóttir, we feel like a real international sports team. We have been formally greeted. We have to behave. Everything suddenly feels special. Jakob, shy at such occasions, maunders a few words in response and everyone goes their separate ways. Darren and Derick disappear to select the team for the following day's international match. Sadun is not spotted again until the morning. God knows what he's doing – but then, God knows everything, which may not be good news for Sadun. I later ask him why he so often attracts female attention. "Because I don't have a tyre in my ass," is his reply, which is as much sense as I've ever got out of him.

The team is announced overnight. Darren springs a surprise: Prabhath will open the batting, alongside Alex. It's our fourth different opening partnership in four games – and Prabhath, who has never performed the role before, will be our fifth opener this week. It'll be Derick at three, Dushan at four, Lee at five, then Abhi and Jakob as finishers. Nolan and Sadun will take the new ball, Lakmal will bowl his seamers first change, then Prabhath and David will send down their spinners. Dushan, who has had to bowl in all three friendly games, has a sore back, and it's agreed he will only bowl in an emergency (which, to my mind, means he will surely bowl).

Our 50-over fixture against Switzerland has many benefactors, not least our hundreds of donors and sponsors, many of whom turn up to watch, sporting their Iceland cricket jerseys. We have been granted the use of the handsome cricket field at St George's College in Weybridge, just outside London, by the headmistress, Rachel Owens. It's a fine setting for a first international cricket match, and Mrs Owens seems as delighted to be hosting it as we are to be playing here.

131

We have also been offered, during our Twitter build-up, the services of Iain O'Brien, a retired international cricketer, as a consultant coach and mentor. It's quite a coup. Between 2005 and 2009, he made 36 appearances for New Zealand during a 167-match professional career. A right-handed fast bowler, he claimed the wickets of many of the greats: Michael Clarke, Matthew Hayden, Michael Hussey and Ricky Ponting of Australia; Alastair Cook, Kevin Pietersen, Andrew Strauss and Michael Vaughan of England; M. S. Dhoni, Rahul Dravid, Virender Sehwag and Sachin Tendulkar of India; Misbah-ul-Haq and Mohammad Yousuf of Pakistan; Hashim Amla and Jacques Kallis of South Africa; Mahela Jayawardene of Sri Lanka; and Chris Gayle of the West Indies. This is one seriously accomplished cricketer.

What's more, he's driven down from Derbyshire – for free. Retired cricketers are very fond of saying "I think it's time I gave something back to the game", but this usually means signing a lucrative commentary box deal or starting a profit-making coaching academy. O'Brien genuinely wants to help. And he is first at the ground. When I introduce him to everyone, he takes pains to reassure Darren he won't be treading on his toes, changing his plans or undermining him. He's there to add insight and value. "Even if all you want me to do is take catching practice, I'm just happy to be here," he says. O'Brien has, astutely, judged that this is the biggest day of Darren's coaching career, and doesn't want to steal his thunder.

Switzerland has a long cricketing history. Maybe not as long as Iceland's – nearly a millennium shorter, in fact – but the sport is much better established. They have nearly two dozen teams (excluding the somewhat contrived six-a-side tournament, Iceland has just two), with hundreds of children involved. They have been a member of the ICC since 1985 and have been playing international matches since 1990. They may be a minnow compared to England and Australia, but to the Icelanders, Switzerland are a cricketing behemoth. They have played 21 European teams, and 76 international matches in all. They've notched up wins against Austria, Belgium, Bulgaria, Croatia, Czechia, Finland, Luxembourg and Slovenia.

We're obviously going to take one hell of a beating.

Derick wins the toss and, on a perfect pitch, decides Iceland will bat first. This seems like lunacy since it more or less guarantees an early finish after Switzerland bundle us out. I can hardly bear to watch as Alex and Prabhath walk out to open, but I'm going to have to, since I'm updating the ball-by-ball score online. Alex, who faced 34 balls against the Authors without scoring a boundary, sets off like a man possessed, smashing five fours in his first 11 balls. This electric start gives Prabhath time to settle in and, though the scoring slows, the pair put on 32 before Alex plays all round a straight ball from Jai Singh. Derick, who always begins watchfully, focuses on rotating the strike with Prabhath; the left-hand, right-hand combination works well. Prabhath gets a couple of fours away, and though he is bowled by Pardeep Kumar for a fairly pedestrian 24, he has built Iceland a platform. Dushan ambles to the wicket at 67 for 2 in the 14th over – it is always an amble with Dushan – and hoicks a four from his first ball. It's a sign of what's to come. In the 18th over there are two sixes. In the 19th, two fours. Rod Sherrell is hit out of the attack. The total races past 100. Farid Din and Thileepan Rasalingam are brought on, without success. The 150 comes and goes.

Among the Icelanders and their gaggle of new-found local supporters, there seems to be disbelief. This is wonderful, as long as it lasts, but it surely won't. Not much longer. And yet, somehow, it does. Dushan overtakes Derick and passes 50, but Derick soon brings up his own half-century. We pass 200. Derick is stroking the ball into gaps, running hard, frustrating the bowlers. Dushan is standing, hitting, demoralising them. The Icelanders become increasingly raucous. Music is played; dances are danced. And suddenly it strikes me – the disbelief is, and was, all mine. None of my team-mates ever doubted us. They, in their joyous naivety, expected this. While I was studying rankings, looking up historical scores, and worrying about tactics, they were hitting tennis balls for six on ten-metre strips of asphalt. They weren't cricket realists, with all the expectation-management demanded by pragmatism. They were devoted adherents of *petta reddast*: the can-do, don't-worry, it'll-work-out school of thought. "Abhism," as Abhi later modestly renames it.

Derick and Dushan have added 163 when Derick hits a skyer off Adam Pratt and is caught for 61. Darren decides to up the ante and promotes Lakmal as a pinch-hitter. "Give it some welly," is his instruction. Lakmal needs no translation; he is already of like mind and wastes no time in setting about the bowling. The score surges beyond 250 and Dushan cruises through the nineties. He brings up his century, off 87 balls, with his fourth six. It is a dream performance: a hundred on international debut, against a vastly superior team, powered by self-belief and raw ability.

Dushan is finally dismissed by Chris Lodge for 134 off 105 balls, with 12 fours and five sixes – reclaiming his record for the highest innings by an Icelander. Lakmal bludgeons 39; Lee and Jakob are selflessly run out in pursuit of last-minute runs. Iceland's final score is 330 for 7 from 50 overs. It is a huge total, and even I wonder whether Switzerland can chase it down.

Switzerland's top five batters hold the key to the pursuit. They are a formidable quintet: young, fit and experienced in top-level amateur cricket in both Europe and Asia. We have a bunch of tapeball players and two giants of dubious physical fitness. Sadun, whose off-the-field antics have robbed him of sleep and mobility, has managed only nine overs on the tour so far. He is, by most measures, in no fit state to play, let alone bowl a full spell. Nolan, a man of health and discipline, is once again being troubled by his shoulder. It may all come down to the spinners.

In the event, it doesn't. Sadun bowls the first ball of the innings to Aidan Andrews, who's drawn into playing outside off stump, and gets a thick edge to first slip, where Lakmal holds a juggling catch. 0 for 1. In the fourth over, Nolan's inswinger bursts through the defence of star all-rounder Jai Singh. 14 for 2. Five balls later, Sadun induces another edge, from Sathya Narayanan, which Lee pouches behind the wicket. 19 for 3. Matthew Martin counterattacks with a flurry of strokes through the covers off both bowlers. But Stefan Franklin plays back to another inswinger from Nolan and is trapped in front. 45 for 4. Martin's adrenaline pumps too hard and he sets off for a quick single, taking on Alex's arm. A direct hit. 47 for 5. Almost immediately, Sadun gets a ball to nip back and pin Sherrell leg before wicket. 49 for 6. Farid Din finds the boundary off Sadun, but when Rasalingam tries to do the same, he pops up a catch to Derick at mid-on. 64 for 7.

This entire passage of play takes less than an hour. It is fantasy made real, and the mood on the field spins from ecstasy to a surreal, stunned silence. Everybody – on both teams – knows Iceland cannot lose from here. Derick gives Nolan a rest, and brings on Lakmal, but decides to keep Sadun going in the hope that he can claim a five-wicket haul, the bowling equivalent of a batter's hundred. He can't, but his final figures of 4 for 39 from 10 overs represent the performance of his life.

A message is sent out to Derick to give the spinners a chance. We don't need them, of course, but it has occurred to Darren that everyone has played a part with bat or ball, except David. With the match as good as won, Derick will be itching to bring himself on to bowl. David's first over goes for 15, including three wides in his first three balls, then two fours from Kumar. But he soon overcomes his nerves: Kumar heaves to Dushan at midwicket, and Lodge picks out Derick. 104 for 9. The Icelanders can hardly contain themselves. Prabhath and David spin through another four overs. And then, with the final ball of the 27th, David knocks over Pratt's wicket, and Iceland are victorious.

England did not win their first international match. Neither did India. Or New Zealand, Pakistan, South Africa or the West Indies. Iceland did. They scored 330. And bowled out Switzerland for 115. *Half* their score. Lee leads the team in the Viking 'thunderclap' made popular by Iceland's footballers at the 2016 European Championship. Darren, Iain and I go into the car park and, for the benefit of our Twitter followers, film a car crushing a Toblerone in slow motion. Iain then eats it. The Toblerone, not the car. By the end of the day, we have 10,000 Twitter followers. More than Spain. More than Malaysia, whose population is 33 million – a hundred times greater than Iceland's.

It's just as well we have so many supporters. We had originally planned to play two T20 games against Switzerland on the Sunday but, owing to a rescheduling of the Swiss players' flight home, that plan was scotched. At a loss for a solution, I turned to Iain with the idea of staging an end-of-tour benefit match, to beef up our development funds (the income won't be there for ever, I reasoned, so we ought to make the most of the attention while we have it). I'd hit upon the idea of auctioning places in a Rest of the World XI, to play Iceland in two games on the Sunday. Iain has volunteered to captain, and a clothing manufacturer, Serious Sport, has agreed to provide personalised kits for his team.

It's a neat little package. You get to play with an international cricketer, against an international team, and gain a new and unique cricket kit into the bargain. The ten places are snapped up, putting another £1,000 into the kitty. In the event, 'Rest of the World' proves a misnomer. Our opponents are from Kent, Lancashire, Middlesex, Durham, Somerset and Sussex, so it's more an English counties' team. The presence of Iain as a New Zealander (even though he now lives in Derbyshire) gives the eleven its world flavour.

The Icelanders are a bit nonplussed by the whole thing; their tour, in spirit, came to an end the previous day. They are content enough to go along with things, as long as I do the work. But steady, match-threatening rain sets in and, in desperation, I turn to Twitter again to see if anyone can lend us an indoor sports hall. A school in Ascot, not far away, steps in to help, and the travelling Icelandic cricket circus decamps. It's a primary school, and the hall is tiny, but it's a case of beggars not being choosers.

We decide to play two games. The first uses the English Cricket Board's newly devised 100-ball format; the second will be a T10. The ECB have recently announced 100-ball innings as the basis for their new flagship competition and have met with almost universal derision. Trial matches will be played in Nottingham in September, so I decide to steal a march on the ECB: the first 100-ball cricket match is played between Iceland and a Rest of the World XI at Lambrook School on Sunday 29 July 2018.

We field the same team that beat Switzerland, but with me replacing Nolan, whose shoulder could do with a rest. Derick generously hands me the captaincy. I decide that, in the first game, we'll give the Rest of the World XI a chance – they have, after all, paid a grand to be here – and in the second, we'll assert our superiority and crush them.

I lose the toss, and Iain puts Iceland in to bat. My first decision is to reverse the batting order, to offer our guests some early hope. Everything goes to plan. Their bowlers chip away, dismissing me, David and Prabhath easily enough, but Sadun makes merry, pinging the ball around for 33, the highest score of his life. Given the length and depth of his hedonism during last night's celebrations, I'm surprised he can stand up, let alone see the ball. When he departs, Iceland are 77 for 5. An unintended outcome of reversing the batting is that Jakob and Abhi, the middle-order run-gatherers, are still in the middle-order. Iain brings himself on to bowl, and quickly sends Jakob's stumps flying with a searing, inswinging yorker. On seeing this, Abhi quickly undoes his leg pads and inverts them, so the upper part, which usually guards the knee, flaps down over his shoes. His esoteric plan to guard against Iain's yorkers doesn't end there. It also involves waving his bat at Iain, walking down the pitch at him, and dishing out some verbals. Iain can't have been sledged like this since he played Australia. And, somehow, Abhi's antics pay off. He swipes a couple of sixes and makes 21. With five overs to go, Iceland are 93 for 8, but Lee, Derick and Dushan boost the total rapidly. Iain gives all his players a bowl, and Dushan launches five sixes in the last two overs. Our eventual total is 173 for 9 from 100 balls.

There's a certain knack to captaining a friendly game against an unknown team who are weaker than you. I've learned it, and honed it, over my years with the Adhocs. The first thing to do is to get yourself into a position of control, without dominating too early. The Rest of the World XI will have felt pretty good when they had us eight down, but our final score is imposing. Now we must stage-manage things in the field. That involves bringing the opposition close to our total, while retaining the option to win the game when we decide to. In short: you aim for victory by the smallest possible margin.

In this case, it's easy, because we have a host of quality bowlers who don't need to bowl. Instead, I restrict the attack to Lee, Alex, Jakob, Abhi and me. Iain hits a cameo of 14, before being bowled by a beautiful inswinger from Jakob, but the principal honours go to Toby Goodman, a teacher from Bath, who bashes 66. The game goes to the final ball, from which a single run is required. Abhi fields brilliantly off his own bowling, and his throw to the non-striker's end finds the batter short by about a metre. The Icelanders leap and holler in jubilation – but so do the Rest of the World players. The umpire says "not out". It's the wrong call (the video footage proves that) but a great victory for public relations. We've made a lot of people, who have travelled a long way to play us, very happy. Abhi is all for remonstrating with the umpire, but I manage to restrain him: "We beat Switzerland yesterday. Let our guests have their moment. And then let's flatten them."

And flatten them we do. Though I captain the 10-over game, I play little part. Instead, I use the full power of our resources (which necessarily involves me not bowling). Iain hits an unbeaten 23, including three big sixes off David, but the Rest of the World XI muster only 93 for 6. It is not enough – nowhere near – and we charge to victory for the loss of only two wickets. Abhi gets the better of Iain again, and Jakob, our chairman, hits the winning run. It's a fitting end to a thrilling, satisfying tour.

Later in August, after all the hangovers have passed, the long-delayed final of the Summer Solstice Sixes is held. Sadun and the Sri Lankans lead Hafnarfjörður to victory against Derick's skilful but underpowered Garðabær. The season seems to have finished, but Abhi is immensely keen for us to visit Prague again. Darren and I can't see the point. We've elevated ourselves beyond participation in club tournaments overseas, haven't we? Shouldn't we now be focusing on cricket that strengthens the Iceland team, and raises its profile? It falls to Jakob, as chairman, to arbitrate and – ever the diplomat – he calls a members' vote. The majority decide we shouldn't undertake the tour, but Abhi, declaring that the votes of any members who haven't previously toured Prague are void, presses ahead regardless.

It's our third Pepsi Cup and follows a near-identical pattern to the first two. The squad is unchanged from the previous year: David, Leslie and Prabhath are again unavailable, which means there are only 11 players, but it's a solid enough team. In fact, with Chamley and Keenan back in place of Alex and me, we're arguably stronger than we were in England. For this reason, the results are a let-down. Yet again, Iceland manage only two wins in the group stage, and advance to the fifth-place play-off. And once more, we lose it. There are no centuries, this time, to balm the sting of underachievement. The only enduring happy memory is of Abhi, struggling to grip the ball when bowling in prolonged drizzle, deciding to use the umpire's trousers – without asking – as a towel. The umpire goes bananas.

The Volcanic Ashes resume in October, and Reykjavík level the series by winning the third and fourth games. The fourth features a classic instance of Abhism: as Kópavogur captain, he finds he has a weak team, so press-gangs Reykjavík's three best batters to play for him. Reykjavík are thrashed by their own players, but the ICA retrospectively awards their runs – and the match – to Reykjavík. Kópavogur clinch December's low-scoring decider and reclaim the title of indoor champions.

At the ICA's end-of-season meeting, my role as secretary is made formal. Jakob steps down as chairman, and Derick as captain. Nolan is appointed to both roles, unifying them for the first time since Anil Thapa's tenure came to an end in 2014. Nolan seems a good fit in both positions: like Jakob, he is statesmanlike, and a peacekeeper; like Derick, his thoughts on the game are respected by the players. He's enthusiastic about growing the profile of Icelandic cricket still further, and approves another round of crowdfunding and publicity for the 2019 season. His decision comes just in time for another unexpected opportunity.

X

INDIA

KINGS XI PUNJAB MIGHT SIGN ICELANDIC SPINNER

The franchise, which is currently fifth in the table and captained by Indian spinner Ravichandran Ashwin, called Kató a "mystery spinner" as he bowls what is called the "fífl" or backspin.

Kató Jónsson, a spinner from the Nordic country, is all set to undergo a trial with Indian Premier League side Kings XI Punjab on Monday. If everything goes well, he could become the first man from the country to play in the IPL.

"This is what the IPL is all about," said Kings CEO Satish Menon to the official team website. "This proves that cricket is truly a global sport that knows no boundaries. To have a cricketer from Iceland in the league would be historic and a testament to our belief that opportunity doesn't discriminate."

The New Indian Express, 1 April 2019

I'd always been terrified of visiting India. I suffer from chronic anxiety, which manifests itself as nausea. And the thing that makes me most anxious is the thought of being sick. Without wanting to get so deep into details that I force you to slam the book shut, if I think I'm going to throw up, I get anxious, which makes me think I'm going to throw up. It's no more pleasant to experience than it is to read about. And it is generally held that a European visiting India has a pretty decent chance of being sick at some stage. Throw in the unfamiliar environment, the heat, and the thought of being thousands of miles from home, and you have the perfect combination for really, really not wanting to go to India. For many years, even the thought of going would turn me green. Some may sympathise, but more have told me it's pathetic and wimpy – it has helped end relationships – but nonetheless, there it is. That's anxiety.

When the invitation arrives, in March 2019, to speak about Icelandic cricket at the annual Playwrite sports literature festival in Chandigarh, I'm as flattered as I am petrified. It comes from Chitranjan Agarwal, an accountant and sports fanatic, who wants me to take the stage alongside veteran cricket broadcaster Charu Sharma, and former India captain Bishan Bedi.

"Can we have you come over and speak about cricket in Iceland? We promise to show you an IPL game as well!"

Everything about the invitation is enticing, but my anxiety implores me not to go. I need an excuse. I tell Chitranjan I can't afford to go – but to my surprise and alarm he offers to cover nearly all the trip expenses. This is not the kind of help I need. Still, I reassure myself, there's no way the ICA will stump up the rest. Just to send the social media guy to India, for a bit of publicity? No way.

Unfortunately, Nolan – keen to be democratic and open-minded – decides to put the question to the rest of the committee and finds Abhi in the midst of one of his big-ideas-to-take-over-the-world seizures. Abhi persuades Nolan to put up the money, on the (obviously ludicrous) assumption that my visiting a small literary festival in northern India will put Icelandic cricket on the map, once and for all.

I am faced with no alternative than to accept. By coincidence or design – I never find out which – on the eve of my departure, I am contacted by the social media manager at Kings XI Punjab, an IPL team based in Chandigarh. I'd call him my opposite number, but his 2.1 million followers dwarf our meagre 10,000. The Kings are a huge, multi-million dollar organisation, owned by four superstars of Indian business and entertainment: investment banker Mohit Burman, businessman Karan Paul, industrialist Ness Wadia and actress Preity Zinta. And someone at the Kings has decided to blow a few notes on an April Fools' Day prank – which is why their digital guy, Raghu Venkatraman, has landed in my inbox as I pack my linen suit and my Xanax.

April Fools' Day pranks are rarely funny, and the 'humorous' announcement from a well-known corporation is usually at the very bottom of the barrel. When Raghu tells me he'd like my help to put together an amusing press release, announcing that an Icelandic cricketer is travelling to India for trials with the Kings, my initial reaction is to recoil. Such jokes are pretty lame. They usually involve the announcement of some unlikely new initiative, with an anagram of 'April Fool' unsubtly worked in, for the benefit of the one or two readers who haven't immediately got the 'joke' (our marketing manager, Flora Pilo, says she is looking forward to the installation of the new paper seating).

I am not keen, but reply to Raghu with as much courtesy as I can muster, saying I'll go along with it if we can actually film my arrival, showing me meeting the players and training in the nets – a hoax so neatly planned and executed that nobody will be sure they're being pranked. To my immense surprise, he agrees.

Raghu and I create Kató Jónsson, an Icelandic spin bowler in his mid-thirties – late in his cricketing life – who has a 'mystery ball'. Fans of T20 cricket, from the kid in the stands to the media multinational, are a sucker for a mystery ball. And, without too much stretching of the imagination, I can play the part. I am a spin bowler. I have a mystery ball: my backspinner. My first name is, in fact, Kató, a name approved by the Icelandic naming committee, and my Icelandic patronym is Jónsson, my father being Jon – though he is from Weston-super-Mare in Somerset, rather than the West Fjords of Iceland. Pity.

By the time I set off, Raghu has approached the Kings' CEO, Satish Menon, and head coach, Mike Hesson, and obtained their approval to play a prank on the entire team – and the Indian sporting press. I will attend the training session at Mohali Stadium, ahead of the team's match against Delhi Capitals; the coach will introduce me to the rest of the squad as a triallist; I will bowl in the nets until they realise something is up. The news of the trial will be circulated among the press.

By the time my plane is airborne, I'm in a tumult of thoughts of heat and bacteria, bowling and vomiting. I keep telling myself it's just a long weekend. It will be over before I have time to throw up.

I travel via London, Dubai and Delhi, and arrive in Chandigarh at lunch-time on Saturday, though my body has long since given up keeping the hours. The Playwrite organisers have everything in hand: a group of university students are whisking delegates away from the airport with impressive efficiency, and within moments I'm zipping along the streets of the city, en route to the Union Territory State Guest House. This is, I'm informed, a private hotel exclusively for visiting government officials and dignitaries. It's comfortable, clean, and the air conditioning is noisy but effective.

The outdoor temperature is quite bearable, and the city's traffic no more deserving of a bad reputation than anywhere in, say, southern Italy. There are a couple of hours before the evening reception, so I have a brief nap, having attempted – with little success – to practise the Indian method with regard to lavatorial hygiene, there being no toilet paper in the bathroom.

When dusk falls, I turn down the offer of transportation and elect to walk to the Chandigarh Golf Club, where the Playwrite committee have laid on food and drinks. It's 500 metres at the most, a pleasant walk down Vigyan Path, one of the city's innumerable tree-lined streets. At the party, I'm introduced to Chitranjan, his co-organiser Vivek Atray, and Thums Up, the Indian version of Coca-Cola (perhaps, as a teetotaller, I find such meetings more significant than others). The food is vegetarian, and delicious. Of course, everybody wants to know about Icelandic cricket, and various agents and publishers press for a book – this book.

After breakfast the following morning, I am driven a couple of miles east, to the Lalit, Chandigarh's most luxurious and exclusive hotel. We pass through several checkpoints, which seems a bit much for a literary festival, but it soon becomes clear that the security isn't for Playwrite, but for the Kings and Capitals cricket teams, who have just arrived to begin their preparation for tomorrow's game. It occurs to me that I ought to do likewise, and Vivek promises to take me somewhere to loosen up tomorrow.

Once I'm on stage, a degree of impostor syndrome kicks in. I'm not overawed by Charu Sharma – he is, after all, just another cricket broadcaster – but I feel a bit of a fraud sharing a platform with Bishan Bedi. This man played 77 times for India; he took 1,631 professional wickets, for heaven's sake. I once bowled one ball to Lawrence Prittipaul (98 appearances for Hampshire), and he hit it for four. In such company, it's a lot easier to listen than to speak, and I speak only when spoken to. I've ridden here on a wave of bluff and bluster, Icelandic cricket's stock in trade. That's how Ragnar ended up on Sky Sports News, and it's how I've found myself addressing a national sports conference alongside a *real* international legend. When does the joke end?

Not soon, obviously. The worst is yet to come. Lunch at the Lalit is an odyssey of flavours – there are even meat dishes – each more delectable than the last. I could eat here for ever. The crowning glory is *gulab jamun*, sweet fried dumplings infused with saffron, syrup and cardamom. They're incredibly moreish. I lose myself in them.

I'm awoken from my sticky-mouthed reverie by a tap on the shoulder. A swarthy, portly, dishevelled figure introduces himself as Raghu, the Kings' social media guy. Everything's ready, he says, for the hoax.

"I've figured it all out with the CEO and coach," he tells me. "You'll go to Mohali Stadium and put on an official training kit. We'll take you over to the nets, and you'll bowl at this 18-year-old we signed this season. He's been told to make you look good. Mike Hesson will be watching you, and will notice your mystery ball, and will start saying stuff like 'this is good, we can use this' until the other players start taking notice."

I feel a jolt of something coursing through my arms. It feels like anxiety, though it could be sugar.

"So, what is this mystery ball?" Raghu asks.

I give him the potted version of my cricketing history. When the story comes to the backspinner, we decide that Kató Jónsson, my alter ego, should be the innovator of this 'new' variation. Bertie Bosanquet devised the googly, Jack Iverson invented the carrom ball, Saqlain Mushtaq gave us the doosra – so Jónsson will pioneer the backspinner. It's revisionist history, given the ball's true age, but such is the spirit of our time. Nat Sciver-Brunt brought back the draw shot, in which the batter hits the ball through his or her legs: now it is the "natmeg". Kevin Pietersen is credited with the popularisation of the switch hit, but Mushtaq Mohammad was certainly batting wrong-handed in the 1960s. Why shouldn't the backspinner be a modern Icelander's invention? We even come up with an appropriate name for it: the *fífl* ('fool').

The ICA help out, too. Anticipating a wave of online searches for 'Kató Jónsson', they change the name on my player profile web page to 'Kató Abrilgabb Jónsson' – Aprilgabb means April Fool – to provide the amateur sleuths with the confirmation they're seeking. The rest is easy. Jónsson needs to be able to speak Icelandic, which I can, and also English with an Icelandic accent, which I can.

Raghu leads me to the Lalit's laundry room, to make sure I have all the right kit. I'm given the trademark red trousers, a training shirt and my official Kings playing jersey, though I haven't been given the jersey number I requested (11), because Mohammed Shami already wears it. There also appears to be a cap for me, monogrammed "KL", presumably standing for Kings' Lions (the team logo features a lion, as a tenuous but non-imperial reference to a 'king').

A car arrives to return me to the guest house, but I ask to be dropped off at Sukhna Lake, and walk back along the shore. Families are out, playing and picnicking, enjoying the warm Sunday afternoon. When I reach my room, I lay out my kit, with a mixture of pride and trepidation. Another wrestle with the lavatory hose. Another nap.

When I wake, it's dark, and late. I'm starving. I take a long walk into the city centre, in search of butter paneer, the great Punjabi delicacy. The locals tell me that Goldie's Roost in Sector 8 is the place to go at this time of night, but I get a bit of a surprise when I reach it. It's little more than a kiosk, with a single table and two chairs. Still, I order butter paneer, plus a few *gulab jamun*, and re-enter my waking dream of sugar, butter and cream. Next morning, I change into my official teamwear, and am met at reception by Vivek, who takes me to a local school playing field to warm up. This turns out to be a mistake, as we are soon the attention of a dozen eager children, who've assumed I am a real celebrity – a real cricketer – who's come to surprise them for a photo call. Even after I bowl a couple of revealingly bad deliveries to Vivek, they are undeterred, and further practice becomes impossible. I'm bundled back into the car, taken to Mohali Stadium, and delivered into the hands of Raghu.

Raghu is accompanied by a small army of media guys, wielding lights, cameras and clipboards. It's a million-dollar corporation, I reason, so its entourage must be substantial. We march across the field – the training area is on the other side of the ground, behind the stands – and I am videoed and photographed from all angles.

As we reach the practice nets, a shortish, sprightly man approaches. He is a little older than me, but similarly bedecked in training kit, and stretches out his hand. It is Mike Hesson, the team coach.

"Kato! Great to see you! Kato. Am I saying that right?"

Is he already making a show for the cameras? I take a deep breath.

"No, actually it's Kató." A rounded 'o'. My best Icelandic accent. "With an ó at the end."

Hesson laughs.

"Ha, you're okay mate, don't worry." He lowers his voice. "I know your name's really Kit."

I'm about to tell him no, it's really Kató, but decide not to complicate the situation. I ask him if he's up to speed on the plan.

"Yeah," Hesson replies. "We're gonna get you in the nets, and you're gonna bowl at this kid we have, Prabhsimran Singh, and we're gonna have a look at you."

"Well, yes. But you know who I am, and what I'm doing here?"

"Sure. All the way from Iceland. Glad you made it."

Wait. He's in on it, isn't he? I look at the photographers and cameras. Then I steal a glance at Raghu.

"This is your in-house media team, right?"

"Nah," says Raghu. "We issued the press release about an hour ago. These guys are from News18 Punjab."

So this is local television. Hesson is already in character. Not just a top-drawer coach, but a first-rate method actor. He's in performance mode – though the spell nearly breaks when he notices I'm not wearing shoes.

"You don't have any spikes?" he asks.

I want to reply "of course not, I came here to speak at a literary festival, and haven't played cricket for six months", but in the present circumstances this seems unwise.

An assistant coach is dispatched to the changing room and returns bearing a pair of size elevens.

"These are Andrew Tye's," says Hesson.

"Won't he need them?"

"Nah. He's not playing today. You're replacing him."

The cameras press closer.

The next thing to draw Hesson's attention is my midriff. He eyes it critically.

"Are you sure you're fit to play?"

This is a cruel blow. I weigh 75 kilograms. I haven't drunk alcohol for 20 years, and my stomach sticks out a couple of centimetres at most. But the Kings jerseys are so tight, I look about four months pregnant.

"You might wanna suck that in," Hesson whispers.

Into the nets we go.

I've never heard of Prabhsimran Singh. The teenager is from Patiala, 45 miles south-west of Chandigarh, and is considered a star of the future. He reeled off centuries for Punjab Under-16s and Under-19s, and was selected for the India Under-19s' tour to Sri Lanka during the winter, when he signed his first professional contracts – for the Punjab state team, then the Kings. Still, I've never heard of him. And, as the youngest member of the squad, it falls to him to play stooge to my masquerade.

Hesson tells the other pros I've just stepped off the plane, and I bowl as though I were still on it. My first ball is an off-side half-tracker: Prabhsimran bunts it gently back. It's okay, I reassure myself – that was just a loosener. But, to my horror, Hesson launches into his act.

"Ooooh, hello!" he exclaims, immediately attracting the interest of Mujeeb Zadran and Murugan Ashwin, the team's second and third-ranked spinners (their captain and principal spinner, Ravichandran Ashwin, is not at training; neither is their superstar batter, Chris Gayle).

My second ball doesn't bounce at all. Prabhsimran summons all his powers of self-restraint and defends again.

Hesson sucks air in through his teeth. "Hey, we could use a bit of this!"

I am mortified. I can bowl a lot better than this.

"Give me a minute," I plead.

But Hesson has already committed himself to purring and simpering over my long-hops and full-tosses. One by one, the pros saunter over to take a look. Sam Curran, England all-rounder. David Miller, South Africa batter. Mohammed Shami, India fast bowler. I start to warm up a little, and settle into a slightly more convincing spell of straight half-volleys, all of which Prabhsimran dutifully blocks, but this improvement comes too late to impress Hesson, who has been called over to the cameras to talk about his potential new signing. As soon as his back is turned, Prabhsimran spanks my bowling to kingdom come. Punjabi television thus broadcasts a remarkable interview in which the Kings coach speaks rapturously about his new signing while, behind him, an 18-year-old with no IPL appearances gives the newcomer the hiding of his life. I pray Prabhsimran becomes the next Tendulkar. At least then I'll be able to claim I kept him tied down for a while.

The media team are keen to film me meeting my new team-mates but, perhaps not surprisingly given how I've bowled, most are reluctant to be associated with me. I am asked to make conversation with Ankit Rajpoot, a painfully thin youngster about 15 years my junior. I ask him, in a heavy Icelandic accent, how he is enjoying school and whether he's pleased with the outcome of his diet. There is laughter from behind the camera, and Rajpoot giggles his way through his answers.

Next I meet Hardus Viljoen, a South African bowler who had, in 2017, forsaken the chance of national honours in his home country in favour of a contract with Derbyshire. This required an effective rejection of his nationality, and the assumption of British resident status. Earlier this year, he reversed the decision, and returned to the South African fold. I suggest to Viljoen that if I play well enough, I will be recognised as Punjabi, can sign as a local player, and move to India permanently. Viljoen doesn't think this is likely.

"But it worked for you in England," I counter.

Rather than punch me in the face, Viljoen roars with laughter. The press, amused and satisfied, down their cameras and depart. Hesson admits his April Fools' Day prank to the players, and it's agreed I should be 'signed'.

A quick call to Menon obtains his assent to announce my signing to the press. Raghu and the social media team take me back to the main field and ask me to do a piece to camera, thanking the Kings for recruiting me.

This is what I come up with:

Icelandic: Hey everybody. My name's Kató Jónsson, from Iceland, and I'm here at the PCA – the Punjab Cricket Association. Welcome to Chandigarh. Only they say it's not actually Chandigarh I came to, it's Mohali, so I don't know how that works. I travelled here for thirty hours, to come from Iceland to India. It's a bit hot. When I left it was −1°C, and here it is about 30. *[I lift a desk fan to my face]* Anyway, they gave me a trial. The coach, his name is *[Icelandic: What's his name again?]* Mike Hesson. Don't worry, I'd never heard of him either. He gave me a trial to bowl six balls at India's Under-19 captain, and they have not seen anything like it. I have bowled this new ball, this mystery ball called the *fifl*. It's the 'backspinner'. And I think there are places for spin bowlers from Iceland to play in

Kings XI Punjab. I am not so good as the captain, Ravichandran Ashwin, who is a very good player. But they play two spinners, so they will pick me too. The coach said to me, you are 39, how are you fit? I said it's true, I cannot really move. I cannot run, only walk. So I am at least fitter than Chris Gayle. He has to be a batter because he's not fit enough to do anything else. You see, this is a team for everyone. They even took a man from South Africa, his name is Hardus Viljoen, and one day he decided to be English, so just like that he was English. It's not difficult for him to play, so for me it will not be difficult. I have told them I am Indian now. And I did not travel here thirty hours just to eat butter paneer. I will now make a special message for Icelanders. *Icelandic: Okay, so people in India say playing cricket for money is every man's dream. Err, no! Cricket may be the dream for Indians, but not for Icelanders. I don't even play cricket. I've never played cricket. This is all a big misunderstanding. Help me. HELP ME.*

I'm invited back to the Lalit to hang out with the team before the match. The media get there first. Hesson, it transpires, has published photos of him and me talking, with the comment: "Serious talent. Keep an eye out for Kató Jónsson." And that's exactly what the press pack is doing. Tongues are wagging, fingers tapping. There is speculation that I might be selected in tonight's team.

Behind the security cordon, the players sit around, bored and aimless. Most retreat to their rooms. I can't, because I don't have one; I don't even have anywhere to change out of my training kit. So I amble about, feeling somewhat out of place. Suddenly there's a buzz, and a path clears through the crowd. Chris Gayle swaggers through, in a flowing silk dressing gown, the kind a heavyweight boxer wears on the way to the ring for a title fight. A gaggle of acolytes attend him closely; none are instantly identifiable as cricket people, and none are less than a foot shorter than Gayle. He's sporting a pair of gold-edged sunglasses so enormous they could double as solar panels. Raghu tells me Gayle didn't go to training this morning because he has a bad back.

Sam Curran is the only player in the restaurant, eating a salad, drinking tea, absorbed in thought. He looks so forlorn I have an impulse to join him, but I check it. He's half my age. What am I going to say? "Hello, young fellow. My name's Kit. I'm the one who was pretending to be an Icelandic mystery spinner at training earlier, but I'm not really. I'm an English travel agent and cricket commentator. Well, it's been a pleasure to meet you. See you around." No, I think I'd better spare us both that conversation.

Raghu beckons me to the front of the hotel, to meet Menon. The boss is deep in conversation with Ravichandran Ashwin, his captain, but when I'm brought forward, he's delighted to see me.

"Have you had a good day?" he asks.

"It's been quite an experience," I answer.

"Sorry not to have said hello at lunch. I nearly came over, but you were mainlining *gulab jamun* and looked so happy, I didn't want to disturb you."

He tells me the national news media have been all over the story. But Raghu interjects with some bad news: the press have started putting two and two together. *The Hindu*, *The Times of India* and *The New Indian Express* have taken their stories down. Menon looks downcast. I have the impression the whole stunt was his idea in the first place.

"We will have to give them something more," he says. "I'll tell them you are playing tonight."

Ashwin raises an eyebrow. He's been in meetings all day, and wasn't at training, and isn't up to speed. Menon puts him in the picture.

"You should show Ashwin this mystery ball," he says. So I do. I show the world's greatest spin bowler the backspinner. He shows me the grip for the doosra. It is then agreed – I don't know how seriously – that he will deliver the *fifi* first ball this evening.

I walk back towards the lobby but am accosted.

"Excuse me, sir? "

I turn round and see three young lads in replica Kings' Lions jerseys. They point at my training kit.

"You are the player from Iceland? Welcome to Punjab. Can we take a selfie with you?"

I see no reason why they shouldn't. The boys withdraw, satisfied, but are immediately replaced by another three.

"Sir, can we take a selfie with you?"

I agree again. And, over the next hour, I realise why the players stay on their side of the cordon. The press of selfie-takers and autograph-hunters is relentless. A couple of teenagers are desperate to show me a drawing they have made of a pretty woman. I ask who it is, and they laugh.

"You don't know?"

I admit I don't.

"It's Preity Zinta!" they cackle. They regard me as though I'm from another planet – which I am, more or less.

"Who's Preity Zinta?"

"She is your boss, sir. She is paying your wages!"

They are waiting for her to arrive at the Lalit, so they can present her with the portrait. She has owned the team for 12 years. She must have hundreds of portraits.

I meet about two hundred admiring fans. An hour is about the right amount of time to be famous, I reckon. Any longer would be exhausting.

Game time draws near. Hesson has decided it would be a step too far to put me on the team bus. Instead, I'm to travel with Menon in his limousine. As we hurtle through the darkening streets, I record some video on my phone.

"Mr Menon, do you have a few words for people who think Kató Jónsson is not real?"

"Oh, he's certainly real," confirms Menon. "He's very much on the roster. And not just that, he's going to open the bowling today."

I post the video on Twitter, and the Kings retweet it with a quote from Menon: "This is what the IPL is all about. This proves that cricket is truly a global sport that knows no boundaries." By the time we reach Mohali, *The Hindu*, *The Times of India* and *The New Indian Express* have put the story back online.

On arrival at the stadium, of course, the jig is up. Instead of joining the players in the dug-out, I am ushered into Menon's private box, accompanied by Raghu, a bevy of immaculate waiting staff and – joy of joys – several hundred *gulab jamun*. I learn that Gayle really is injured and hasn't even come to the ground. The man charged with the task of replacing him at the top of the batting order is Curran. Curran! No wonder he was looking so grave earlier. Tye is, as promised, omitted from the team. So are Rajpoot and Prabhsimran, who has to wait a few more weeks until his debut. We're playing three spinners: Ravichandran Ashwin and Mujeeb Zadran are no surprise, but I really did think I might have got the nod ahead of Murugan Ashwin.

The Kings get off to a flyer, with Curran smashing 20 from 10 balls, but the Capitals' seam bowlers fight back and restrict the total to 166 for 9. Miller top-scores with a rapid 43. The Capitals' openers are a formidable pair: Prithvi Shaw (134 on Test debut for India) and Shikhar Dhawan (187 on Test debut for India). Maybe it's just as well I'm not opening the bowling. Ravichandran Ashwin delivers the first ball to Shaw and – it can't be – it is! It's the backspinner, the *fifi*, and Shaw edges it to the wicketkeeper! There it is, crystal clear, on the replay. Never in my life have I been as proud as I am right now, of my young protégé. What a man. What a player. He *listens*, that's his greatest asset. He respects age and experience. He'll go far, that young man.

What's more, he bowls it again – at least I think he does – to dismiss Dhawan for 30, halfway through the innings. But the Capitals recover from their early setbacks, and eventually need just 23 runs from 21 balls with three wickets down. What follows is extraordinary. In the space of 17 balls, the Kings take the remaining seven wickets for the addition of eight runs; Curran claims a hat-trick and is named player of the match. It's one of the great games of the IPL season.

At the end, I'm taken down to the boundary's edge where the media scrum is at its most frenetic. Zinta flounces and prances about, hugging the players, taking selfies with her superstars, and furiously berating any of the menial staff who displease her – not least when it transpires her bottle of water is not cold enough. Cameras and interviewers shove their way around, like they did this morning, but my photograph is not taken, nor my words recorded. The bubble has burst.

Hesson and several of the players wander over to say goodbye. Ravichandran Ashwin nods at me but says nothing. Viljoen and Rajpoot shake my hand. I thank Tye for the loan of his boots. It's the first he's heard of it. Last of all comes K. L. Rahul, another star of the national team. I'm surprised he's noticed me.

He asks to have his cap back.

The cap with "KL" on it.

Oops.

XI

GROUNDED

A traveler cannot bring a better burden on the road than plenty of wisdom, nor no worse a burden than too much alcohol.

The Poetic Edda, c. 10th century

Everything is ticking over nicely in Iceland. My Indian sojourn has brought in more Twitter followers and more donations. Reykjavík win the 2019 Volcanic Ashes 4–1 indoors at Kórinn, with all the national squad players in decent form. Ahead of the third game, I am contacted by a young Icelander, on behalf of a group of 11 local students who have resolved to play a different sport every weekend in the year. He wonders if there's any chance they could try cricket. Reykjavík and Kópavogur are both substantially short for the match, so they all get a game. They're all given a chance to do something, too: four of them score 6, and one makes an impressive unbeaten 9, narrowly failing to get Kópavogur over the line in a pulsating finish. Four of them take wickets, including Marteinn Jóhannesson, whose 3 for 14 for Reykjavík are the best bowling figures of the day. He's a natural. It's wonderful to have a full complement of -ssons in an Icelandic cricket match – but next week it's rugby, apparently, and we never see them again.

Nolan has big plans for his tenure as chairman. He wants us to host multiple touring teams during the season, as we had in 2015 and 2017. For my part, I've started to look into how we might gain ICC membership. Until now, the Icelandic Cricket Association has existed contentedly outside the auspices of the ICC, and enjoyed its freedom to muck around, and troll the big nations. But I've begun to feel we're too insular. Put the Summer Solstice Sixes aside, and we're really just a single cricket club with two teams, Reykjavík and Kópavogur; everything from kits to selection is organised centrally.

My feeling is that the ICA should become an umbrella organisation, overseeing the activities of several independent clubs. To join the ICC, we need eight clubs – or four, each with two teams – plus women's cricket, junior cricket, and training for ground staff, scorers and umpires. We also need two grounds, each with a playing area dedicated to cricket.

It would be a mammoth undertaking. The five team identities we used for the Summer Solstice Sixes are a sound basis for expansion, but we're some way off having enough players even for three full teams on any given day. Women and children's cricket don't exist at all – though we do have the Reddit money set aside.

I decide the first thing to do is find a proper ground. Clearly, Kórinn has got to go – it's an artificial football pitch, there's no disguising that. It may work for an annual indoor tournament, but if we're going to have full-size outdoor games, we need real grass.

Starting with a satellite photograph of Reykjavík and the surrounding area, I mark all the areas of green space large enough for a cricket field. There are 38. Jakob and I resolve to visit them all. A dozen are non-starters, being too marshy or sloping. Another 20 are grass training pitches belonging to the main football clubs. They might let us hire them, but there's no way they'd let us install anything permanent. In any case, these are being replaced, one by one, with artificial surfaces like the one at Kórinn. That leaves six. One is inside a running track – like the fields used at Stykkishólmur and Laugardalur by Ragnar and his pioneers in the early 2000s – which seems to be asking for trouble with hard cricket balls flying around. Klambratún park, home of Icelandic cricket from 2005 to 2014, presents a similar problem, and a return to Tungubakkavellir is ruled out since it's too far away.

Three options remain. First, Jakob and I visit Hamranesvöllur, on the heath above Hafnarfjörður. The setting is stunning and, though the field's marked out for football, it looks like there would be little competition for use of the field. But there are no facilities at all – not even shelter. Next, we check out Valhúsahæð, on an exposed hill in the middle of Seltjarnarnes. It, too, is a striking location, and marked out for football, but it's exceptionally windy, and surrounded by residents' back gardens. I can't imagine the locals taking too kindly to us.

So we are down to one location, and neither Jakob nor I hold out much hope. It's Víðistaðatún, the small park in Hafnarfjörður where the pioneers organised the Icelandic Cricket Cup match in 2002. It looked pretty in the photograph I showed to Ragnar, but the grass seemed very long and lush, and the playing area small. There seems to be a scout hut next to it, too – there'll surely be kids camping and whatnot all summer.

But the moment Víðistaðatún comes into view, we know we've found our promised land. All the basic requisites are there. The turf is soft, even and surprisingly bouncy. Our cricket ball makes a 'thunk' sound every time it lands; there must be voids under the surface, which means it'll drain well. It's small, but not impossibly so: there's room for an even 45-metre boundary. And it's the only flat, decent-sized area of grass in the capital area without football markings all over it.

The surroundings are perfect, too. The field is an elongated pentagon, bounded by paths on all sides. On its north edge is a lava flow, dating from a pre-settlement eruption. Local legend says that invisible elves dwell there, and are not to be disturbed, though the elves appear to have permitted the construction of a handy little path through the lava to a grocery store. To the north-east is Víðistaðakirkja, a striking church built in the 1980s, with columns mimicking the natural basalt found all over Iceland. To the south-east are a children's playground and barbecue area, which might help us attract families. The south-west edge is bordered by a row of birch and separated by a small wall from a little campsite. If a touring team wanted to visit us on a shoestring, this would be ideal. The campsite's run by the scouting organisation, who also have a hostel and car park, on a ridge above the ground to the north-west. At the foot of the ridge, abutting the field, is a pavilion with kitchen, toilets and shower rooms, belonging to the campsite. It has benches and a canopy – it could double as a cricket pavilion at any club ground in the world.

Hafnarfjörður town council have, with a degree of grandiosity, designated Víðistaðatún an 'International Sculpture Park', with artworks from Finland, France, Germany, Japan, Mexico and Switzerland. The most prominent, set on the ridge overlooking the ground, is Timo Solin's 'The Watch', a sentry fashioned from blue twisted metal, standing guard on what might easily pass for an enormous cricket wicket. Even the park's name seems symbolic: Víðistaðatún means 'meadow of the willow', the very wood from which cricket bats are made.

I rush to call Nolan, to tell him I've found our new ground (neglecting to mention it was really Ragnar who found it, 17 years previously). My dream is to turn Víðistaðatún into the home of

Icelandic cricket. The scouting organisation and Hafnarfjörður council are soon brought on board: the scouts agree to let us use the pavilion, and the council provide a garage for storage. Now all we need is something to store in it.

I press the committee to buy a mower and roller (surprisingly, persuading them to cough up the money is the hardest mission I've yet accomplished at the ICA). I arrange for a white-line marker and boundary flags to be sent from England. Then, somewhat jammily, I enter a competition to win a new roll-out cricket pitch – and win it. The cost of importing it seems prohibitive, but Ambassador Nevin saves the day by pulling a few diplomatic strings.

On a whim, I look up the world's northernmost cricket ground, and discover it's in Umeå, Sweden. Its latitude is 63.84N, some 16 miles further south than Víðistaðatún (64.07N). Since we're going to break a world record, I invite the Prime Minster of Iceland, Katrín Jakobsdóttir, to open the ground. Not only does she accept, she agrees to face a ceremonial 'first ball', which Ambassador Nevin – a cricketer, remember – will bowl.

A suitable opposition, with fame and prestige, needs to be invited, and there is an English team that fits the bill. The Captain Scott Invitation XI are the subject of not one, but two books: *Rain Men*, concerning their travails as an English social team, and *Penguins Stopped Play*, about their tours abroad. All things considered, the 'Scotties' are (with apologies to the Authors) the most famous social cricket team in England. They're only too happy to come, of course, and the gala opening is arranged for the afternoon of 26 May 2019. Our team will play as the Prime Minister's XI, and our visitors will be the British Ambassador's XI.

As soon it's known the Prime Minister is coming, we are inundated with offers of help. Abhi decides to run a prize raffle, and a couple of dozen local companies pitch in. Vala Yates, a singer-songwriter, offers to sing the national anthem a cappella. A British tea company sponsors a traditional tea tent. The only fly in the ointment is when Nolan announces he won't be there – he's taking a family holiday the same weekend.

In the absence of our chairman, the meeting and greeting falls to me. Katrín Jakobsdóttir arrives with several television crews in tow, and delivers a handsome address to open the ground. Ambassador

Nevin and I reply in kind. My delight at shaking hands with the Prime Minister, and presenting her with an Iceland jersey, turns to awe when she strides out to the pitch to face the first ball.

Politicians usually fall on their face when they have to do a sporty photoshoot. It's a notorious pitfall, but the Prime Minister is determined and game. She's dressed for the occasion, with trainers, miniskirt and an authentic cricket sweater, and dons an Iceland Cricket baseball cap without a moment's worry about her hair. How many prime ministers would dive in with such zest? She settles at the crease – adopting a distinctly open stance – and says her only preparation was being told to keep a straight bat (she doesn't). Eight players take up catching positions behind her, to make sure they're on camera. Ambassador Nevin bowls a gentle ball on a length, and she biffs it back past him. She raises her bat to acknowledge hearty applause, then sticks around for a few more hits. Ambassador Nevin, despite his cricketing prowess, comes off second best: one wayward delivery hits a television camera right in the lens.

Everybody stands for the national anthem, and the Icelanders take the field. Apart from me and Prabhath, who sit out the game, all the regulars play a part. Sadun and Lakmal's seamers make early inroads, Chamley and Lee take turns at keeping wicket, Abhi is electric in the field and the spin of David and Keenan keeps the visitors quiet: their final score is 109 for 7. We expect to knock the runs off easily but, after a solid start from Leslie and Derick, and some pyrotechnics from Dushan, we run into trouble. When Sammy is dismissed first ball, we are 60 for 4. But Leslie is still there and finds a useful ally in Jakob; not for the first time, it falls to the two accumulators to get us out of a hole dug by the big-hitters. They turn the game around, adding 51, and bringing the Prime Minister's XI victory over the British Ambassador's XI by six wickets.

The Scotties manage a win in the second game, against a deliberately weakened Iceland team (I'm in it), thus setting up a decider. Dushan is its star, blasting an unbeaten 107 from 57 balls, then bowling a fiery spell to hold the tourists off.

In June, the World Cup is staged in England, which provides an abundance of fodder for Twitter. I boost Iceland Cricket's followers – and infamy – by taking the piss out of everyone and everything. We're the worst national team in the world, so it's all 'punching up', right?

Wrong. England thrash Afghanistan, whose star player, Rashid Khan – arguably the finest spin bowler at the World Cup – concedes over 100 runs. Feigning ignorance, I tweet congratulations to him for bringing up the milestone. His Sussex team-mates, led by England legend Jofra Archer, start a Twitter pile-on. It seems a little harsh: Rashid Khan is a superstar, a millionaire; my joke is so silly, so puerile. The accusations of Islamophobia seem excessive, as do the death threats. But it's the performative outrage that rankles me most. A BBC colleague calls me – to my face – "the most hated man on Twitter". Another broadcaster, Alan Wilkins, tweets to his 250,000 followers that Icelandic cricket has "lost a lot of friends", which is peculiar given he's never previously shown any interest in us.

Later in the month, we are visited by Sutton Benger, a village team from Wiltshire. They play a match at midnight on the Summer Solstice – the first time such a game has taken place in Iceland since the Effigies came in 2003 – and manage to win it. They retire to the campsite full of confidence and cheer. They don't realise they've played an under-strength, 'good hosts' side. The full national team spanks them in the remaining games. The following weekend, Reykjavík come out on top in the Summer Solstice Sixes and, having also won the Volcanic Ashes, become the first team to do the double.

The summer sweeps on. We make headlines again when I suggest on Twitter that we want to give citizenship to Ambati Rayudu, a promising batter who's just been dropped from the India squad. The attention is not quite worth it: we receive scores of requests for Icelandic citizenship from enthusiastic Indians. An Indian cricket academy arranges to play us – and would be by far the toughest opponents to reach our shores – but the Danish Embassy in India (we don't have one there) refuses them Icelandic visas.

The team who visit us in August are plenty strong enough, though. The trouble with touring teams is that they tend to come for a long weekend. All the strongest clubs put out league sides on a Saturday, meaning the cricketers who come to Iceland are usually of the weaker, social sort. Iceland are now unbeaten in seven home series, dating back to 2015; the last English team to win a series in Iceland was the Effigies, 16 years ago. Americans and Australians have won – even Scots – but Iceland is a fortress to the English.

Wessex Old Boys have better prospects. They're a once-a-year team of old university friends, but they all play league cricket regularly, and have taken time off from their respective clubs to form a touring side. We agree to play two games, of 20 and 40 overs, and our half-strength side loses off the final ball of the first. That sets up a crucial match next day, which the full-strength team seems to be bossing when Wessex slip to 10 for 3, but they dig in, seeing off the spinners and cashing in against the rest. Their captain scores an imperious 80 in a total of 181 for 7. Unlike our guests, we're not used to planning a chase lasting more than 20 overs, and the target presents a stiff challenge. Leslie, Derick and Chamley are swept aside, and we're soon up against it. Though Lee and Abhi both make runs, no one takes control of the pursuit, and we fall well short.

After our great progress in England the previous summer, the ICA has accepted an invitation from Malta to participate in an international T20 tournament in October. The show is back on the road. Darren flies over to Iceland for some preparation with the boys and strategic meetings with Nolan. Darren promises to send a training plan to Iceland every week, to get them ready for the tour. It all works well for the first week – Lee calls it "the most productive training session I've ever had in Iceland" – but Darren is told not to send any more. I worry there's a disconnection between the team's preparations in Iceland, and the coach's planning in England. I try to interpose myself in the breach, but it's not really my place. I just hope they're not practising on a tennis court again.

The usual squad is assembled, and we learn from the Maltese that we're to compete for the Valletta Cup, with Czechia, Hungary and Malta. We'll be playing at Marsa, a smart private ground, and an impressive place to play, if the photographs on its website are anything to go by. We expect to give a good account of ourselves, after our success in England in 2018. Nolan seems a natural captain. He's older than the other players and regarded as something of a father figure. He's trusted. He's knowledgeable. When he speaks, everybody listens. He even manages to hook us up with the services of a professional physiotherapist, Kieren Lock, who'll accompany us throughout the tour.

Once again, things go wrong before we even set off. For the third time, Chamley is unable to obtain a visa. To make matters worse, David, who is close to completing his doctorate, has been called up to attend the Arctic Circle Assembly, whatever that is. I'm brought in, but it's too late to call up Alex Sabelli, so we embark with just 13 players – hardly ideal for four matches under the Mediterranean sun.

The problems continue when we reach Malta. The tournament entry fee suddenly doubles – I've apparently made the error of liaising with a notoriously slippery individual, a known bullshitter, who is now *persona non grata* in Maltese cricketing circles. I had spent weeks fruitlessly pressing this man to commit the arrangements to paper but eventually decided to take it on trust. Big mistake. The new head honcho, Indika Thilan, is a bright and credible doctor from the general hospital, and I wish I'd dealt with him from the start. He's hugely apologetic, but there's not much we can do.

The Marsa ground itself is dog-eared and unkempt and bears little resemblance to its photographs. There are several large, bare areas on the outfield, and the artificial pitch is of the older type – an astroturf mat laid on concrete. I figure there won't be much in it for the bowlers, but Darren insists a total of 120 will be highly competitive.

The final shock comes when Darren and Nolan install themselves in the hotel's rooftop lounge, and call the players in one by one, to tell them their roles for the tournament. Initially, there are few surprises. Leslie and Derick to open. Keenan, Dushan and Lee in the middle order. Abhi and Jakob at six and seven, to run the ball around and finish the job. That, we assume, leaves us with six bowling options: Nolan, Lakmal, Sadun and Dushan as seamers, then spin from Prabhath and Keenan. Sammy's the reserve batter, and I'm the back-up bowler. But Darren tells Nolan he's decided that Lakmal won't bowl: he doesn't get much lateral movement on the ball, and will be easy prey for the batters. The news comes as a shock. Whether it's a sound cricketing move or not, the impact on the team is substantial. Lakmal's a wholehearted and popular player, and there is widespread sorrow that he's been disappointed. Nolan is obviously torn. He believes in Lakmal, and wants him to bowl, but feels he must back Darren up.

Our opening game is against Malta. Nolan wins the toss, and decides we'll bat first, aiming for Darren's magic 120. Leslie finds it tough going, and is first out, for a tortured 4. Derick and Lee rebuild with a stand of 64: Derick, lacking fluency, nudges the ball into gaps while Lee goes for his shots. He bludgeons a couple of huge sixes and reaches 49 before he is brilliantly stumped going for another big hit. No more boundaries are found after Lee goes, and though Keenan watchfully sees out the innings, our total of 107 for 5 looks undercooked. Malta make a sprightly start, taking advantage of the 'powerplay' rule that restricts the fielding side to two men on the boundary for the first six overs. They are 50 for 1 when the restriction is relaxed but, curiously, Nolan sticks with two boundary fielders for the rest of the innings. And though Malta's batters struggle a little against Keenan and Prabhath's spin, there are easy runs whenever they loft the ball over the infield, which is often. Nolan's shoulder starts to hurt, so he thoughtfully gives an over to Lakmal, but our hosts stroll home with a couple of overs to spare.

That evening, at our team dinner, Darren reminds Nolan that he can put five fielders in the outfield from the seventh over onwards – and should. Every captain in every T20 game does so. But Nolan shrugs the advice off. "I just had a hunch," he replies.

Darren decides to drop Leslie for the Hungary match (the first of two games the next day), which Leslie takes badly. I feel for him – over the last year or so, we've become firm friends, and I've spent more time with him than any other member of the team. He's a wise man, a sensitive soul, and a shrewd thinker when it comes to cricket. Unlike me, he knows when to keep his peace and let things wash over him. I'd have given him a second chance before shaking up the batting order.

There's no way Sadun can play twice in a day, so I'm brought in as a third spinner. Sammy and I are presented with our international caps before the toss: Nolan wins and again decides to bat. Once more, runs prove hard to come by. Our opponents are, once more, vastly better in the field, and restrict us to just five boundaries in our 20 overs. Derick and Keenan take us to 70 for 2, but there's another collapse. Sammy hits his first ball in international cricket for four, much to everyone's delight, and is third-highest scorer, with 14. We finish on 108 for 8.

Darren urges Nolan to open with a slow bowler, and Prabhath is entrusted with the task. It proves an inspired move: he takes two wickets in successive balls and puts Hungary on the back foot. Their two biggest hitters, Zeeshan Kukhihel and Zahir Mohammed, are now in the middle. As soon as the powerplay ends, Nolan decides to go for an all-out spin attack: me at one end, and Keenan at the other.

Suddenly, but not for the first time, I'm anxious. I haven't bowled on an artificial pitch for 20 years, and I feel quite out of place. Nolan distracts me from my nerves by inviting me to set my own field, and I immediately send five men out to the boundary: deep backward square, deep midwicket, long-on (I imagine they'll go after me), long-off and deep cover. I keep midwicket, extra-cover, backward point and fine leg in the ring.

My first delivery is a half-volley on middle and leg: no trouble for Zahir, who hits it high and long over the midwicket boundary, into a building site. The ball is lost. I manage to drag the length back for the second delivery, but it's on leg stump and Zahir clips a single to the on side. My third delivery is straighter, but too full, and Zeeshan picks up a run to long-on. Next, I try the backspinner, which slips out of my fingers and darts to the leg side – but so does Zahir, who's hit on the pad. A dot ball. Maybe I'll finish the over strongly, I think. No such luck: Zahir smashes the fifth ball into the building site again.

"Too straight, Kit!" yells Lee. "Outside off, mate!"

The advice comes somewhat late, but he's right, and I should have figured it out myself. Full and straight works well enough in club cricket, but batters at this level think nothing of it. I have to adjust my aim.

My final delivery is a decent backspinner. It dips onto a good length, a little outside off stump, and Zahir shapes to cut it. But the ball jumps a touch, precisely as I want it to, and snicks the bat on the way through to Lee – who drops the catch.

With a moan of anguish, I sink to my haunches. The umpire hands me my cap with a look of sympathy. As the field changes for the end of the over, Lee passes me. I catch his eye, half-expecting him to say sorry.

Instead, he shrugs. "Shit ball."

International cricket is tougher than I am.

Zeeshan adds a six off Keenan, who exacts a swift revenge by pinning him in front next ball. I long to bowl at the new batsman, but the brutal truth is I haven't earned another over. Nolan brings himself on in my place, and Zahir goes into overdrive, banging five more sixes before holing out off Prabhath, who returns figures of 4 for 22. It's not enough. After 15 overs, Hungary are all but home, and this time Abhi, rather than Lakmal, is given a bonus bowl before our defeat is completed.

An old university friend of mine used to say, "If you can't be the best, be the worst." With this adage in mind, as soon as I leave the field, I announce my international retirement. Given the length and quality of my career, I can hardly expect a guard of honour or standing ovation; I'm sure Nolan and Darren are relieved get rid of the dead wood. My international career, from debut to official retirement, has lasted two hours and 40 minutes. It's a world record that will take some beating. Exercising rare tact and self-restraint, I decide not to inform my team-mates of my achievement.

The mood in the camp remains positive. Two defeats are a blow, but all four teams are to play in the semi-finals, so we can lose every group match and still win the tournament. If we can finish strongly, as we did in England, we can pull off a surprise. Sadun replaces me for the afternoon game, against Czechia, and Sammy's cameo looks like keeping Leslie on the bench until Jakob pretends to be exhausted and incapable of playing. The idea is preposterous – he's the fittest man on the team by a distance – but so obviously designed to accommodate Leslie, nobody dares question his magnanimous gesture.

Czechia win the toss and elect to bat, and we hope we can keep them to something around 100, which seems to be the limit of our batters' capabilities. We look like doing it when Keenan's spell of 4 for 19 reduces them to 77 for 6, but their lower order gets them out of trouble. Prevented by his shoulder injury from bowling himself, and forbidden from calling on Lakmal, Nolan asks Derick to bowl his off-breaks, with disastrous consequences. Fours and sixes fly from the bat – and Iceland still don't have five men on the boundary. Derick and Lee exhort Nolan to make changes, to do *something*, but he is hesitant, almost frozen. Lee ends up calling the shots from behind the wicket. Spirits sink, the atmosphere sours, and Darren loses his cool. The Czechs rack up 155 for 7.

There's not much talking during the break. Keenan, one of our best batters, tells Darren he's tired and wants to bat down the order. Darren puts him down at number eleven. Leslie, opening the batting, makes a seven-ball duck, Lee lasts two deliveries, and Sammy is run out without facing. We meander aimlessly to 72 for 7.

Being Icelandic, by residency if not by birth, we refrain from discussing our problems that evening. We go for dinner on an old pirate ship and focus on drinking rather than analysis. Lee steals a raw fish from the kitchen and prances about, hitting everyone round the head with it. Sadun, never far from the brink of violence, does not take kindly to the assault, and tells Lee he'll kill him, there and then, if he does it again. Nolan decides he'd better intervene, and edges towards Lee with hands raised and voice lowered: the clown whisperer.

"Now, Lee. Let's calm down. You're not going to hit anyone else with that fish," he purrs, in his smoothest diplomatic voice.

"Wrong!" yells Lee, landing a slap across Nolan's chops that would make Monty Python proud.

One way or another, we have broken the ice. And the mood improves further when I tell the team we're playing third-ranked Hungary in our semi-final tomorrow. As the lowest-placed team, we should be playing the group leader, but the tournament structure was agreed, well in advance, with first playing second and third playing fourth. Dr Thilan calls me after dinner, pointing out the error and asking Iceland to consent to a correction to the schedule. Naturally, I refuse.

Darren makes one change for the semi-final, dropping Leslie for the second time in the week, and bringing back Jakob. We lose the toss and are asked to bat, and Darren sends out Lee and Keenan, our fourth opening pair in as many games – this is becoming a Darren hallmark. Both are soon run out, and the Bandaras don't last long either. But Sammy keeps his end up, buying Derick time to compile a crucial 61, which lifts Iceland to 125 for 8. It's our highest score of the tournament, and we all feel we have a real chance, now we've warmed up. Unfortunately for us, so have Hungary. Zeeshan batters 55 from 26 balls, repeatedly driving Sadun for four.

"Why don't you bowl short, buddy? He keeps driving you," exhorts Nolan.

"I try! I try! But is not possible. I not know why!" replies Sadun, helplessly.

Though Keenan eventually removes Zeeshan, we have no more luck, and the Hungarians power to their target. We've come fourth, by a distance, and all we've won is the trophy for 'Best Behaved Team', which we give to Abhi.

The coronavirus reaches Iceland on 28 February 2020. As with any external shock to a small, geographically-isolated population, the pandemic hits hard and fast. In a desperate attempt to limit the sweep of the virus, Katrín Jakobsdóttir's government quarantines the public and raises the drawbridge. There are no public gatherings – which spells the end for Icelandic cricket, for the best part of eighteen months. And there are no flights – which spells the end for my travel company, for good.

Hardly anyone thinks of sport in Iceland during the dark times. All the Icelandic Cricket Association's initiatives – the international team, the domestic tournaments, the tours and tourists, the children's programmes, the ICC membership application – are mothballed indefinitely. Within a few short years, it's the second time I've found myself suddenly out of work. Just as it was taking off, my second career has fallen to earth with a thump. Still, the Icelanders and I are grateful to survive the pandemic, and though misfortune dictates our paths will not cross again, except as friends, there is light at the end of the tunnel for us all.

Taking a distinctly long shot, I apply for the position of assistant editor at *Wisden Cricketers' Almanack*. To my immense surprise – and inexpressible delight – I'm successful. It is, without exaggeration, my dream job. Around the same time, the leadership of the Icelandic Cricket Association is passed to Bala Kamallakharan, a venture capitalist and cricket nut with a keen eye for business. Nolan becomes the national team coach, and David takes on the social media role. They prove to be far more than safe hands. Within a couple of years, five clubs are officially constituted, more than 100 players are on the books, and the Twitter following has risen beyond 100,000. By that measure, the Iceland cricket team can lay claim to be the most popular amateur sports team in the world.

Given how it all started, in Ragnar's uncle's apartment, it is extraordinary to think that such fame has been achieved by the Iceland cricket team. It's just the sort of thing that makes the native Icelanders proud. Or at least it would – if only they knew.

INDEX OF NORSE CRICKETERS

Arnbjörn Ásbrandsson (Eyrbyggja saga) and his brother, Björn, are so good, they aren't allowed to play on the same team.

Ásbjörn Þórsteinsson (Gísli's saga) is felled by his opponent, Þórdur, who then calls him a "cesspool pig".

Auðun of Viðidalur (Grettir's saga) dislikes being hit when batting, so knees the bowler, Grettir, in the balls.

Blíg Þorláksson (Eyrbyggja saga) is not allowed to play on account of his aggressive temperament.

Björn Ásbrandsson (Eyrbyggja saga) and his brother, Ásbjörn, are so good, they aren't allowed to play on the same team.

Börk Þórsteinsson (Gísli's saga) can't get Þórstein out by conventional means, so breaks his bat in two.

Egil Skallagrímsson (Egil's saga) has trouble batting, being seven years old, so murders his opponent, Grím.

Gísli Súrsson (Gísli's saga) bowls violently and floors Þórgrím, who'd killed his brother, and follows up with a neat poem.

Grettir Ásmundsson (Grettir's saga) hits Auðun, the batter, in the head with the ball; Auðun knees him in the balls.

Grím Heggson † (Egil's saga) does well with the ball and shows off until his opponent, Egil, plunges an axe into his brain.

Grímur the elder (Hálfdán's saga) bats well in front of a king and queen, and later murders the king.

Grímur the younger (Hálfdán's saga), during a game, persuades the queen to leave her matrimonial bed later that night.

Gull-Þórir Oddsson (Gull-Þórir's saga) is an accomplished player, but not a popular choice as captain.

Hallur Guðmundsson (Laxdæla saga) gives a long-retired player, Kjartan, to the opposition, then loses to them.

Hörður Grímkelsson (Hörður's saga) delivers an inspiring team talk, after which his men literally slay the opposition.

Hrafn the Flemish (Hrólf's saga) is a brutal bowler who, like his brother Krákur, imposes terror on every batter; he is tripped by a spectator and retaliates by breaking his neck.

Hrólf Sturlaugsson (Hrólf's saga) gets called upon to rescue his team from two brutal Flemish bowlers, Hrafn and Krákur.

Ingólfur Þorsteinnsson (Hallfreður's saga) quits a game in order to flirt with a female spectator for the rest of the day.

Jökull Holmkelsson (Víglund's saga) hurts the batter, Víglund, but is knocked out in return when he bats.

Kjartan Ólafsson (Laxdæla saga) tells Hallur he hasn't practised for a long time but turns out to the best player.

Kolgrímur Álfsson (Hörður's saga) plans to rig a game, but six of his men are killed by Hörður's team.

Krákur the Flemish (Hrólf's saga) is a brutal bowler who, like his brother Hrafn, imposes terror on every batter who faces him.

Ólaf Ólafsson † (Þorstein's saga) is angered by Þórir's tactics and assaults him. Þórir stabs him to death after the close of play.

Stefnir Þorgnason (Hrólf's saga), an immense player, is begged to save his team from the Flemish brothers, Hrafn and Krákur.

Víglund Þórgrímsson (Víglund's saga) is hit on the head by a ball bowled by Jökull but returns the favour the next day.

Þórður Þórðarson (Þórður's saga) knocks his opponent, Ásbjörn, to the ground and calls him a 'cesspool pig'.

Þórir Víkingsson (Þorstein's saga) ends a game by bowling a bye, for which the batter, Ólaf, attacks him. He later stabs Ólaf.

Þórgrím Þorsteinsson (Gísli's saga) gets knocked down twice by a bowler, Gísli, whose brother he's killed.

Þórstein Þórkelsson (Gísli's saga) bats for so long that the bowler, Börk, breaks his bat so Þórstein assaults him.

DISCIPLINARY SUMMARY

Murders during play: 8 (including one spectator).
Murders after play: 3 (including one king).
Deaths in battle after play: 7.
Players injured by the ball: 9.
Assaults by bat: 3.
Assaults by hands: 3.
Assaults by knee to groin: 1.
Assault by poetry: 1.
Incidents of sledging: 1 "cesspool pig", 1 "bum-fluff".
Broken bats: 1.
Post-game head injuries while discussing tactics: 1.

ACKNOWLEDGEMENTS

I would like to thank all those who helped me with the research and production of this book.

The Icelanders: Stebbi Ásmundsson, Dushan Bandara, Lakmal Bandara, Dharmendra Bohra, Keenan Botha, Ólafur Briem, Abhi Chauhan, David Cook, Leslie Dcunha, Derick Deonarain, Chamley Fernando, Sammy Gill, Valur Gunnlaugsson, Keith Hayward, Siggi Jónsson, Ragnar Kristinsson, Ásta Sól Kristjánsdóttir, Sadun Lankathilaka, Simon Minshull, Lee Nelson, Jóhannes Númason, Kári Ólafsson, Stefán Pálsson, Jakob Robertson, Darren Talbot, Anil Thapa, Ólafur Unnarsson, Benedikt G. Waage, Prabhath Weerasooriya, Nolan Williams and Barry Woodrow.

The tourists: Erik Bouwmeester, Derek Braidner, John Clarke, Tim Dellor, Hugh Ellerton, Andrew Imlay, Greg Johnson and Jonathan Rule.

The historians: Jane Gulliford Lowes, Professor Terry Gunnell, Peter Salmon, Dr Bill Short and Dr Bev Thurber.

The media people: Chitranjan Agarwal, Jonathan Agnew, Vivek Atray, Matthew Engel, Bryan Henderson, María Lilja Viðarsdóttir at *Morgunblaðið*, and my publisher, Matt Thacker.

On a personal note, I would like to thank those whose influence on my own cricketing journey got me here: my grandfather Roy Harris, Professor Chris Caseldine, Paul Sherlock, Phil Venier, Andy Hurry, Daniel Norcross, Nigel Henderson, Adam Mountford, George Dobell, my colleagues at *Wisden Cricketers' Almanack*, and Bohdana Ladyrova, without whom I would never have got the job done.